Manual For The

YOUTH
SELF-REPORT

And

PROFILE

Thomas M. Achenbach
Departments of Psychiatry & Psychology
University of Vermont

Craig Edelbrock
Department of Psychiatry
University of Massachusetts

Request for Research and Clinical Papers

The authors would appreciate receiving reports of research and clinical use of the Youth Self-Report and related instruments. Please include author's name, address, and telephone number, as well as all available bibliographic information. Information on ordering this *Manual* and other CBCL materials can be obtained from: Thomas M. Achenbach
Department of Psychiatry
University of Vermont
Burlington, VT 05401

Proper bibliographic citation for this *Manual*:

Achenbach, T.M., & Edelbrock, C. (1987). *Manual for the Youth Self-Report and Profile*. Burlington, VT: University of Vermont Department of Psychiatry.

Related Books

Achenbach, T.M. (1985). *Assessment and taxonomy of child and adolescent psychopathology*. Newbury Park, CA: Sage Publications.

Achenbach, T.M., & Edelbrock, C. (1983). *Manual for the Child Behavior Checklist and Revised Child Behavior Profile*. Burlington, VT: University of Vermont Department of Psychiatry.

Achenbach, T.M., & Edelbrock, C. (1986). *Manual for the Teacher's Report Form and Teacher Version of the Child Behavior Profile*. Burlington, VT: University of Vermont Department of Psychiatry.

Achenbach, T.M., & McConaughy, S.H. (1987). *Empirically-based assessment of child and adolescent psychopathology: Practical applications*. Newbury Park, CA: Sage Publications.

Library of Congress Catalogue Card #: 87-70414
ISBN 0-938565-00-1

Printed in the United States of America 10 9 8 7 6 5 4 3 2 1

USER QUALIFICATIONS

The Youth Self-Report (YSR) is designed to be filled out by youth who are 11 to 18 years old. It can also be administered orally to those who have poor reading skills, as described in Chapter 1. Although the YSR is intended to be self-explanatory for respondents having at least fifth grade reading skills, it is important for the user to introduce the YSR in a tactful and sensitive manner appropriate for the situation. In most situations, an appropriate introduction would be: "We would like you to fill out this form in order to obtain your views of your interests, feelings, and behavior." The respondent should be assured of confidentiality, which should be strictly guarded.

After the YSR is introduced to the respondent, an adult who is familiar with the YSR should remain available to answer any questions that arise. Questions should be answered in a factual and objective manner to help the respondent understand the literal meaning of items, rather than to probe his or her thoughts.

When the YSR has been completed, it can be used as a take-off point for clinical interviewing. The interviewer can ask if the respondent would like to discuss any of the items and can ask for further information on issues raised by the YSR responses. Using the YSR in this fashion requires training and experience in interviewing adolescents. For many adolescents, the YSR is an effective "ice breaker" that stimulates them to talk about their concerns. Clinical use of the YSR requires skills commensurate with at least the Master's degree level in psychology, social work, or special education, or two years of residency in psychiatry.

To make proper use of the YSR scales, the YSR should be scored on the profile appropriate for the respondent's sex. It is also important to compare the results with data from other sources, such as parents, teachers, observations, interviews, standardized tests, and biomedical assessment. The user must therefore have access to multiple sources of information about the respondent and must be trained in the theory and methodology of standardized assessment, as well as in work with adolescents. Relevant graduate training of at least the Master's degree level is usually necessary. No amount of prior training, however, can substitute for professional maturity and a thorough knowledge of the procedures and cautions presented in this *Manual*.

All users should understand that the YSR is designed to obtain self-reports of feelings and behavior in a standardized fashion for comparison with reports by normative groups of 11- to 18-year-olds. No item or score should be automatically equated with any particular diagnosis or inferred disorder. Instead, the responsible professional will integrate self-report data with other types of data in the comprehensive evaluation of adolescents and their families.

PREFACE

This *Manual* is intended to provide basic information needed for understanding and using the Youth Self-Report (YSR) and its scoring profile. The YSR is designed to obtain self-reports on most of the same competencies and problems rated by parents on the Child Behavior Checklist (CBCL) and many of the problems rated by teachers on the Teacher's Report Form (TRF). Although not required for using the YSR or this *Manual*, the *Manual for the Child Behavior Checklist and Revised Child Behavior Profile* (Achenbach & Edelbrock, 1983) presents our conceptual framework, as well as basic technical data for the CBCL. A more extensive presentation of conceptual issues in assessment and taxonomy is provided by Achenbach (1985), while Achenbach and McConaughy (1987) illustrate empirically-based assessment using multiple instruments in diverse cases.

To aid users in moving between the YSR, CBCL, and TRF, the *Manuals* for the three instruments are laid out in a generally parallel fashion. Like the other *Manuals*, this one serves partly as a progress report for an ongoing research program, rather than as a final report on work that has ended. The YSR is one component of an approach that we call *multiaxial empirically-based assessment*, which we will continue to develop. The *Manual* is intended primarily for professionals and trainees concerned with the emotional and behavioral problems of adolescents, including psychologists, psychiatrists, social workers, and special educators. Because not all portions of the *Manual* will be of equal interest to all users, the Reader's Guide following this Preface provides an overview to aid in locating pertinent material.

In preparing this *Manual*, we have benefited greatly from the help of Dr. Stephanie McConaughy, who has critiqued the manuscript and provided feedback from her own work. We are also indebted to G. Dana Baron, Cathleen Gent, Catherine Howell, and Matthew Tarran for their computer work, to Ellen Richards for her help in obtaining the normative data, and to Judy Ewell and Kathleen Talbert for preparing the manuscript. Much of the research reported here was supported by grants from the W. T. Grant Foundation, the Spencer Foundation, and NIMH Grant No. 40305, which we deeply appreciate.

READER'S GUIDE

CONTENTS

LIST OF FIGURES

LIST OF TABLES

Chapter 1
The Youth Self-Report Form of the Child Behavior Checklist

The Youth Self-Report (YSR) is designed to obtain 11- to 18-year-olds' reports of their own competencies and problems in a standardized format. It includes many of the same items as the Child Behavior Checklist (CBCL) for completion by parents and the Teacher's Report Form (TRF) for completion by teachers.

Even though the YSR, CBCL, and TRF ask many similar questions of parents, teachers, and adolescents, the answers may differ. Numerous studies have shown only modest correlations between ratings of adolescents by parents, teachers, mental health workers, observers, peers, and the subjects themselves. (Achenbach, McConaughy, & Howell, 1987, present meta-analyses of studies reporting correlations between these different raters.)

Discrepancies between reports by different informants do not necessarily mean that one informant is right and the other is wrong. Neither does it mean that both are unreliable. Instead, it may mean that the adolescent behaves differently in their presence, that they differ in their effects on the adolescent, or that their standards of judgment differ.

The subjects themselves should, of course, have the most complete knowledge of their own behavior across situations. This makes them potentially important contributors to the assessment process. For young children, social and cognitive immaturity limit their ability to recall and report the way they feel and behave in different situations, thus limiting the use of rating forms for self-reports. Adolescents, however, are better able to provide self-ratings. The YSR was therefore developed to obtain adolescents' views of their own functioning in a way that would permit comparison with reports by others, such as their parents and teachers.

Even though adolescents' presumably know their own behavior better than others do, this does not mean that adolescents' self-reports should be the ultimate criterion for accuracy. What they report about themselves is apt to be affected by their recall at that moment, how they construe the questions, their candor, and their judgment of their own functioning. Owing to any of these factors, adolescents may fail to report things about themselves that are reported by other informants, such as parents or teachers. Adolescents' self-reports are not, therefore, intrinsically better than reports by others who know them. Instead, adolescents' self-reports are one facet of assessment that should include reports by informants who see the adolescents in different contexts, as well as by the adolescents themselves.

Disagreements between the informants should not be regarded as error, but as potentially useful information about differences in the behavior observed and/or differences in judgments of similar behavior. The YSR thus provides a means for comparing adolescents' self-ratings on many of the same items as parents rate on the CBCL and teachers rate on the TRF, but the YSR is not a substitute for reports by other informants.

For ages 11 through 16, the CBCL, TRF, and YSR norms make it possible to compare the degree of deviance from normative samples indicated by the parent, teacher, and self reports. Above the age of 16, however, norms were not obtained for parent and teacher reports, because it is difficult to obtain informed reports by parents and teachers on representative samples of 17- and 18-year-olds. Nevertheless, if a parent or teacher is well-informed about a particular 17- or 18-year-old, their reports can be compared with those of the youth on each YSR item that has a counterpart on the CBCL or TRF. (Similar items bear the same numbers on the three forms.) The CBCL and TRF scale norms for ages 12-16 can also be used as rough approximations for judging the degree of deviance indicated by ratings by well-informed parents and teachers of 17- and 18-year-olds.

Figure 1-1 shows the social competence items that appear on pages 1 and 2 of the YSR. These items parallel the competence items of the CBCL except for being worded in the first person and except for the omission of items about special class place-

— for office use only —
IDENTIFICATION #

YOUTH SELF-REPORT FOR AGES 11–18

YOUR AGE	YOUR SEX ☐ Boy ☐ Girl	GRADE IN SCHOOL	YOUR NAME

YOUR RACE ☐ Black ☐ White ☐ Other (specify)	TODAY'S DATE Mo. _____ Date _____ Yr. _____ DATE OF BIRTH Mo. _____ Date _____ Yr. _____	PARENT'S TYPE OF WORK *(Please be specific — for example: auto mechanic, high school teacher, homemaker, laborer, lathe operator, shoe salesman, army sergeant.)* *FATHER'S* TYPE OF WORK: _____ *MOTHER'S* TYPE OF WORK: _____

I. **Please list the sports you most like to take part in.** For example: swimming, baseball, skating, skate boarding, bike riding, fishing, etc.

☐ None

a. _____
b. _____
c. _____

Compared to others of your age, about how much time do you spend in each?

Less Than Average	Average	More Than Average
☐	☐	☐
☐	☐	☐
☐	☐	☐

Compared to others of your age, how well do you do each one?

Below Average	Average	Above Average
☐	☐	☐
☐	☐	☐
☐	☐	☐

II. **Please list your favorite hobbies, activities, and games, other than sports.** For example: cards, books, piano, crafts, etc. (Do not include T.V.)

☐ None

a. _____
b. _____
c. _____

Compared to others of your age, about how much time do you spend in each?

Less Than Average	Average	More Than Average
☐	☐	☐
☐	☐	☐
☐	☐	☐

Compared to others of your age, how well do you do each one?

Below Average	Average	Above Average
☐	☐	☐
☐	☐	☐
☐	☐	☐

III. **Please list any organization, clubs, teams or groups you belong to.**

☐ None

a. _____
b. _____
c. _____

Compared to others of your age, how active are you in each?

Less Active	Average	More Active
☐	☐	☐
☐	☐	☐
☐	☐	☐

IV. **Please list any jobs or chores you have.** For example: Paper route, babysitting, making bed, etc.

☐ None

a. _____
b. _____
c. _____

Compared to others of your age, how well do you carry them out?

Below Average	Average	Above Average
☐	☐	☐
☐	☐	☐
☐	☐	☐

Fig. 1–1. Competence items on Page 1 of the YSR.

V. **1. About how many close friends do you have?** ☐ None ☐ 1 ☐ 2 or 3 ☐ 4 or more

   2. About how many times a week do you do things with them? ☐ less than 1 ☐ 1 or 2 ☐ 3 or more

VI. **Compared to others of your age, how well do you:**

	Worse	About the same	Better
a. Get along with your brothers & sisters?	☐	☐	☐
b. Get along with other kids?	☐	☐	☐
c. Get along with your parents?	☐	☐	☐
d. Do things by yourself?	☐	☐	☐

VII. **Current school performance**

☐ I do not go to school

	Failing	Below Average	Average	Above Average
a. English	☐	☐	☐	☐
b. Math	☐	☐	☐	☐
Other subjects: c. _____	☐	☐	☐	☐
d. _____	☐	☐	☐	☐
e. _____	☐	☐	☐	☐
f. _____	☐	☐	☐	☐
g. _____	☐	☐	☐	☐

Please describe any concerns or problems you have about school

Fig. 1–1 (cont.). Competence items on Page 2 of the YSR.

VIII. Below is a list of items that describe kids. For each item that describes you **now** or **within the past 6 months**, please circle the 2 if the item is **very true** or **often true** of you. Circle the 1 if the item is **somewhat** or **sometimes true** of you. If the item is **not true** of you, circle the 0.

0 = Not True   1 = Somewhat or Sometimes True   2 = Very True or Often True

0 1 2	1. I act too young for my age	0 1 2	40. I hear things that nobody else seems able to hear (describe): _____
0 1 2	2. I have an allergy (describe): _____		
0 1 2	3. I argue a lot	0 1 2 b41. I act without stopping to think
0 1 2	4. I have asthma	0 1 2 42. I like to be alone
0 1 2	5. I act like the opposite sex	0 1 2 43. I lie or cheat
0 1 2 a6. I like animals	0 1 2 44. I bite my fingernails
0 1 2	7. I brag	0 1 2 45. I am nervous or tense
0 1 2	8. I have trouble concentrating or paying attention	0 1 2 46. Parts of my body twitch or make nervous movements (describe):
0 1 2	9. I can't get my mind off certain thoughts (describe): _____	

0 1 2   47. I have nightmares
0 1 2   48. I am not liked by other kids
0 1 2 a49. I can do certain things better than most kids

0 1 2 b 10. I have trouble sitting still
0 1 2 b 11. I'm too dependent on adults
0 1 2   12. I feel lonely
0 1 2   13. I feel confused or in a fog
0 1 2   14. I cry a lot
0 1 2 a 15. I am pretty honest
0 1 2   16. I am mean to others
0 1 2   17. I daydream a lot
0 1 2   18. I deliberately try to hurt or kill myself
0 1 2 b 19. I try to get a lot of attention
0 1 2   20. I destroy my things
0 1 2   21. I destroy things belonging to others
0 1 2   22. I disobey my parents
0 1 2   23. I disobey at school
0 1 2   24. I don't eat as well as I should
0 1 2   25. I don't get along with other kids
0 1 2   26. I don't feel guilty after doing something I shouldn't
0 1 2   27. I am jealous of others
0 1 2 a 28. I am willing to help others when they need help
0 1 2   29. I am afraid of certain animals, situations, or places, other than school (describe):

0 1 2   50. I am too fearful or anxious
0 1 2   51. I feel dizzy
0 1 2   52. I feel too guilty
0 1 2   53. I eat too much
0 1 2   54. I feel overtired
0 1 2   55. I am overweight
56. Physical problems without known medical cause:
0 1 2   a. Aches or pains
0 1 2   b. Headaches
0 1 2   c. Nausea, feel sick
0 1 2   d. Problems with eyes (describe):

0 1 2   e. Rashes or other skin problems
0 1 2   f. Stomachaches or cramps
0 1 2   g. Vomiting, throwing up
0 1 2   h. Other (describe):

0 1 2   30. I am afraid of going to school
0 1 2   31. I am afraid I might think or do something bad
0 1 2   32. I feel that I have to be perfect
0 1 2   33. I feel that no one loves me
0 1 2   34. I feel that others are out to get me
0 1 2   35. I feel worthless or inferior
0 1 2   36. I accidentally get hurt a lot
0 1 2   37. I get in many fights
0 1 2   38. I get teased a lot
0 1 2   39. I hang around with kids who get in trouble

0 1 2   57. I physically attack people
0 1 2 b58. I pick my skin or other parts of my body (describe):

0 1 2 a59. I can be pretty friendly
0 1 2 a60. I like to try new things
0 1 2   61. My school work is poor
0 1 2   62. I am poorly coordinated or clumsy
0 1 2   63. I would rather be with older kids than with kids my own age

PAGE 3   *Please see other side*

Fig. 1-2. Problem items on Page 3 of the YSR. Items marked *a* are socially desirable items that replace CBCL items, while those marked *b* differ slightly from CBCL items.

0 = Not True   1 = Somewhat or Sometimes True   2 = Very True or Often True

0 1 2	64. I would rather be with younger kids than with kids my own age
0 1 2	65. I refuse to talk
0 1 2	66. I repeat certain actions over and over (describe): _____
0 1 2	67. I run away from home
0 1 2	68. I scream a lot
0 1 2	69. I am secretive or keep things to myself
0 1 2	70. I see things that nobody else seems able to see (describe): _____
0 1 2	71. I am self-conscious or easily embarrassed
0 1 2	72. I set fires
0 1 2 a	73. I can work well with my hands
0 1 2	74. I show off or clown
0 1 2	75. I am shy
0 1 2	76. I sleep less than most kids
0 1 2	77. I sleep more than most kids during day and/or night (describe): _____
0 1 2 a	78. I have a good imagination
0 1 2	79. I have a speech problem (describe): _____
0 1 2 a	80. I stand up for my rights
0 1 2	81. I steal things at home
0 1 2	82. I steal things from places other than home
0 1 2	83. I store up things I don't need (describe): _____
0 1 2	84. I do things other people think are strange (describe): _____

0 1 2	85. I have thoughts that other people would think are strange (describe): _____
0 1 2 b	86. I am stubborn
0 1 2	87. My moods or feelings change suddenly
0 1 2 a	88. I enjoy being with other people
0 1 2	89. I am suspicious
0 1 2	90. I swear or use dirty language
0 1 2	91. I think about killing myself
0 1 2 a	92. I like to make others laugh
0 1 2	93. I talk too much
0 1 2	94. I tease others a lot
0 1 2	95. I have a hot temper
0 1 2	96. I think about sex too much
0 1 2	97. I threaten to hurt people
0 1 2 a	98. I like to help others
0 1 2	99. I am too concerned about being neat or clean
0 1 2	100. I have trouble sleeping (describe): _____
0 1 2	101. I cut classes or skip school
0 1 2 b	102. I don't have much energy
0 1 2	103. I am unhappy, sad, or depressed
0 1 2	104. I am louder than other kids
0 1 2	105. I use alcohol or drugs other than for medical conditions (describe):
0 1 2 a	106. I try to be fair to others
0 1 2 a	107. I enjoy a good joke
0 1 2 a	108. I like to take life easy
0 1 2 a	109. I try to help other people when I can
0 1 2	110. I wish I were of the opposite sex
0 1 2	111. I keep from getting involved with others
0 1 2	112. I worry a lot

Please write down anything else that describes your feelings, behavior, or interests

Fig. 1–2 (cont.). Problem items on Page 4 of the YSR. Items marked *a* are socially desirable items that replace CBCL items, while those marked *b* differ slightly from CBCL items.

ment and grade retention, which were deemed inappropriate to ask youth to report about themselves. Page 2 provides space in which the youth is asked to describe any concerns or problems about school. The open-ended responses in this space are often useful as a take-off point for interviews, but they are not scored. Responses to the other items on pages 1 and 2 are scored on the competence scales of the Youth Self-Report Profile, as described in Chapter 2.

Pages 3 and 4 of the YSR (Figure 1-2) list problem items to which the youth responds by circling *0* if the item is *not true*; *1* if the item is *somewhat or sometimes true*; and *2* if the item is *very true or often true*. The 0-1-2 response scale and the problem items without a superscript in Figure 1-2 are the same as on the CBCL, except for being worded in the first person on the YSR. (Achenbach & Edelbrock, 1983, present the rationale for the problem list and response scale.)

The 16 items with superscript *a* in Figure 1-2 are socially desirable items that replace CBCL problem items which were deemed inappropriate to ask adolescents, mostly because they are characteristic of younger ages. The socially desirable items are not scored on the profile. Items with superscript *b* have been altered slightly from the CBCL to make them more suitable for adolescents. A space is also provided on page 4 to "write down anything else that describes your feelings, behavior, or interests." The open-ended responses are useful in the same way as responses to the open-ended item about school on page 2, but they are not scored on the profile. Note that the items on pages 3 and 4 are numbered 1-112, but that Item 56 includes physical problems *a* through *h*, for a total of 119 items. Because 16 of the items are socially desirable characteristics, the total number of specific problem items is 102, plus item 56h, which provides space for listing any physical problems without known medical cause that are not specifically stated in other items. If a respondent circled 2 for all of the 102 specific problem items and 2 for an additional physical problem listed by the respondent, the total score would be $103 \times 2 = 206$.

On several items, the youth is asked to describe the problem in question. This enables the user to avoid scoring problems not properly covered by that item or for which another item is more specific. Examples include *9. I can't get my mind off certain thoughts*; *46. Parts of my body twitch or make nervous movements*; and *66. I repeat certain actions over and over*. On other items, descriptions are requested to enable the user to determine the specific content of the problem the youth is reporting. Examples include *29. I am afraid of certain animals, situations, or places, other than school*; *40. I hear things that nobody else seems able to hear*; *56d. Problems with eyes*; *58. I pick my skin or other parts of my body*; *70. I see things that nobody else seems able to see*; and *105. I use alcohol or drugs other than for medical conditions*. If a youth's description of a problem indicates that the item is scored inappropriately or that the youth scored more than one item for the same problem, only the item that corresponds most precisely to the problem should be counted. (Appendix A provides details of scoring.)

The instructions on page 3 of the YSR state that the ratings should be based on a 6-month period, which is the same as specified for parents' ratings on the CBCL. If a user wishes to obtain reassessments over intervals of less than 6 months, the instructions can be changed to specify shorter periods. For example, if a user wishes to obtain self-ratings before therapy and 3 months later, it is advisable to instruct the youth to base ratings on the previous 3 months each time, so that intervals of the same length are compared.

ADMINISTRATION OF THE YSR

The YSR is designed to be completed by 11- to 18-year-olds having a mental age of at least 10 years and fifth grade reading skills. It is self-explanatory, but someone familiar with the YSR should tell the respondent why it is to be filled out and should be available to answer questions. In most situations, the youth can be told that "We would like you to fill out this form in order to obtain your views of your interests, feelings, and behavior." The respondent should be assured of confidentiality, which should be strictly guarded. Completed forms should not be accessible to unauthorized people. The structured items usually take about 15 minutes to complete, but respondents who write much on the open-ended items may take longer.

If a youth has poor reading skills, the YSR can be administered orally. If there is a question about the youth's reading skills, the interviewer can hand the YSR to the youth while retaining another copy. The interviewer then says, "I'm going to read these questions to you and I'll write down your answers." After the first few questions, respondents who can read well enough will usually start answering the questions without waiting for them to be asked. Questions about items should be answered in a factual manner aimed at helping the youth understand the specific meaning of items, rather than clinically probing the youth's thoughts. If the YSR is administered orally, it should be done in a private location, out of earshot of others.

SUMMARY

The YSR is designed to obtain 11- to 18-year-olds' reports of their competencies on 17 items similar to those of the CBCL and their problems on 103 items similar to those of the CBCL. It provides a basis for comparing adolescents' views of their own functioning with data from other assessment procedures, such as the CBCL and TRF. Discrepancies between reports by different informants can reveal variations in the youth's functioning in the presence of different informants and in their judgments of the youth's competencies and problems. The YSR is designed to be filled out by adolescents who have a mental age of at least 10 years and fifth grade reading skills, but it can also be administered orally. It can be readministered periodically to assess changes in self-reported functioning.

Chapter 2
The Youth Self-Report Profile

As described in Chapter 1, the YSR is designed to obtain adolescents' reports of their own competencies and problems in a standardized format. To compare an adolescent's self-ratings with those obtained for normative groups, the YSR is scored on the YSR Profile. To reflect sex differences, separate versions of the profile have been constructed for boys and girls at ages 11 to 18.

COMPETENCE SCALES

The competence items of the YSR parallel those of the CBCL, except for the omission of structured items for special class placement, grade retention, and other school problems. Items concerning involvement in sports, other recreational activities, and work activities are scored on the Activities scale of the profile in the same manner as on the CBCL profile. Items concerning participation in organizations, number of friends, contacts with friends, how well the youth gets along with others, and how well he/she does things alone are scored on the Social scale, as done on the CBCL profile.

Because the only YSR items scored for school are ratings of performance in academic subjects, there is no point in having a separate scale for school functioning. However, the mean score for performance in academic subjects is added to the scores for the Activities and Social scales to obtain a total competence score. (Detailed hand-scoring instructions are in Appendix A; contact Dr. Achenbach for information on computer-scoring programs.)

The scores for each item and the total competence score are entered on the competence portion of the YSR Profile, as shown in Figure 2-1. To compare a youth's scores for the Activities and Social scales with those obtained by normative samples of the same sex, percentiles can be read from the left

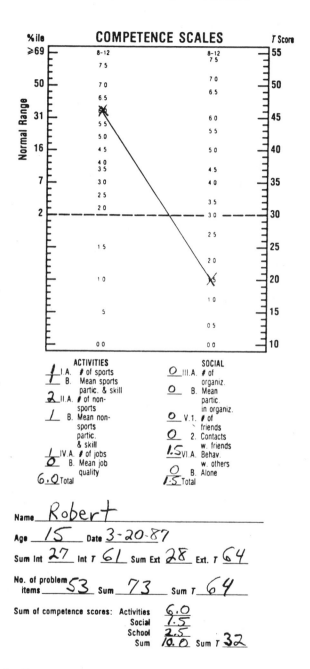

Fig 2–1. Competence portion of a hand-scored YSR profile completed for 15-year-old Robert.

side of the profile and normalized T scores can be read from the right side.

The percentiles on the left side of the profile indicate the percent of adolescents in our normative samples who obtained a score less than or equal to each raw score. The normalized T scores are based on the percentiles of the raw score distribution according to the procedure specified by Abramowitz and Stegun (1968). Unlike ordinary T scores—which transform raw scores in a linear fashion to produce a mean of 50 and standard deviation of 10—normalized T scores are arranged so that a particular T score approximates a particular *percentile* across all scales. This means that normalized T scores do not necessarily have a mean of 50 and standard deviation of 10. Furthermore, following the procedure used for the CBCL competence scales (Achenbach & Edelbrock, 1983), we based T scores on percentiles starting at the 2nd percentile, because normative samples do not contain enough scores below this point to make percentiles a meaningful basis for comparison.

As shown in Figure 2-1, a broken line is printed across the competence scales at the 2nd percentile to indicate the border between the normal and clinical range. Raw scores that were lower than those obtained by 98% of the normative sample (i.e., scores below the 2nd percentile) were assigned T scores from 10 to 29 in equal intervals, as done on the CBCL profile. Following the procedure used on the CBCL profile, we also truncated the top of the competence scales at the 69th percentile. That is, all scores on the Activities and Social scales that were equal to or higher than those obtained by 69% of the normative samples are grouped on the profile at the 69th percentile and are assigned a T score of 55. This was done to prevent overinterpretation of differences between scores that are at the high end of the normal range. As detailed in later sections, the full range of differentiation among scale scores can be retained by using raw scores for statistical analyses, if desired.

A total competence score is computed by summing the total raw scores for the Activities and Social scales, plus the mean score for academic performance. Normalized T scores for each raw total competence score are listed in Appendix A. These T scores are based on percentiles of the raw scores obtained by our normative sample, ranging from the 2nd percentile ($T =$ 30) to the highest possible raw score, which is assigned a T score of 80. Raw scores below the 2nd percentile were divided into equal intervals for assignment to T scores from 10 to 29.

Case example. Robert, a 15-year-old boy whose competence scales are shown in Figure 2-1, obtained a raw score of 6.0 on the Activities scale. By looking to the left side of the profile, we can see that a score of 6.0 is just above the 31st percentile. This means that over 31% of the boys in our normative sample obtained Activities scale scores of 6.0 or less. Robert's Activities score is thus within the normal range for adolescent boys.

On the Social scale, Robert obtained a score of 1.5. By looking at Figure 2-1, we see that a score of 1.5 is well below the broken line that marks the 2nd percentile of the scores for the normative sample of adolescent boys. Because Robert's responses to the Social scale items place him below the scores of 98% of the boys in the normative sample, his social relationships are likely to be an important area of concern.

Robert's self-ratings on performance in academic subjects yielded a mean score of 2.5, which is entered beneath the competence scales, as shown in Figure 2-1. This score is added to the Activities and Social scale scores to obtain a total competence score. Although there is no specific clinical cutoff for the total competence score, Appendix A lists T scores for each total competence score. Robert's total competence raw score of 10.0 is equivalent to a normalized T score of 32, which is at about the 3rd percentile for adolescent boys.

Normative Samples

The percentiles and normalized T scores of the profile were derived from YSRs completed in 1985-86 by 344 boys and 342 girls living in 8 communities of the Worcester, Massachusetts,

metropolitan area. These YSRs were obtained by sending interviewers to 7,884 homes in 263 randomly selected clusters located
in 34 residential census tracts. The census tracts were stratified
by income to yield a sample with similar proportions of lower,
middle, and upper SES families. The interviewers screened
families to identify those having an 11- to 18-year-old adolescent who had not received any mental health services during the
previous 12 months.

If parents granted permission, eligible adolescents were
offered two free movie tickets to complete the YSR and parents
were asked to complete the CBCL. In families with more than
one eligible adolescent, a random number table was used to
select the subject. If the adolescent agreed to participate, the
interviewer gave him/her a copy of the YSR. The interviewer
then read the competence items and the first four problem
items aloud from a second copy of the YSR and recorded the
adolescent's responses. If it was clear that the adolescent could
read well enough, he/she then completed the remaining items
on pages 3 and 4 of the YSR. If reading skills were questionable,
the interviewer continued to read the items aloud and recorded
the responses.

Of the 850 eligible adolescents identified in the survey, 807
completed YSRs, for a completion rate of 94.9% of known
eligibles. (The first 686 YSRs were used to construct the norms,
but the remaining 121 also contributed to the analyses reported
in this *Manual*.) Out of the 7,884 households visited, 81 were
vacant, 313 refused screening, and 217 were not successfully
screened in 5 callbacks, mainly because no resident could be
reached. Of the 7,273 households that were successfully screened, 11.7% had eligible adolescents. If we multiply 11.7% times
the 530 households that were not successfully screened, we
obtain 62 hypothetical adolescents who might have been eligible
but could not be identified. Adding 62 to the 850 identified
eligibles yields 912 as the potential pool of eligibles. Out of this
potential pool of 912, the 807 completed YSRs constitute an
estimated lower bound of 88.5% for the completion rate.

Table 2-1 summarizes the SES and racial distributions of the
normative samples. The SES levels were scored according to
Hollingshead's (1975) 9-step scale for parental occupation, using

the higher status occupation when both parents were wage earners. If an occupation could not be precisely scored on Hollingshead's scale, we used the mean of the two levels that seemed most appropriate. This resulted in some half steps, such as 1.5 and 2.5. For purposes of analysis, we grouped the scores into the three levels shown in Table 2-1.

Table 2-1
Socioeconomic and Racial Distributions
of Normative Samples

	Boys $N = 344$	*Girls* $N = 342$	*Combined*[b] $N = 686$
SES[a]	%	%	%
Upper	35	26	31
Middle	39	43	41
Lower	26	30	28
Mean	5.2	4.8	5.0
SD	2.4	2.3	2.3
Race			
White	79	83	81
Black	18	15	17
Mixed & Other	3	2	3

Note. Because of rounding, columns may not sum to 100%.
[a]Hollingshead (1975) 9-step scale for parental occupation, using the higher status occupation where both parents were wage earners; scores 1-3.5 = Lower; 4-6.5 = Middle; 7-9 = Upper.
[b]Unweighted means of boys and girls.

BEHAVIOR PROBLEM SCALES

Except for the 16 socially desirable items marked with superscript *a* in Figure 1–2, the items on pages 3 and 4 of the YSR are designed to tap specific problems and also to identify syndromes of co-occurring problems, as reported by adolescents. It is important to identify syndromes for the following reasons:

1. Attention cannot be focused simultaneously on each individual problem tapped by the YSR. Aggregation of

co-occurring problems into syndromes enables us to attend to multiple aspects of functioning by chunking many specific items into a few groups.

2. In the assessment of specific problems, measurement error arises from variations in adolescents' recall of particular problems, willingness to acknowledge them, and interpretations of what should be reported in response to each item. Scores for groups of items found to co-occur are potentially more reliable and valid than scores for individual items, each of which is subject to unique sources of measurement error.

3. Problems that co-occur may constitute a class of characteristics that are partially interchangeable with each other. Assessment of each problem separately from the other members of a syndrome may miss variation in the related members of the syndrome.

Referred Samples

To determine which problems occur together to form syndromes, we performed statistical analyses of YSRs completed by adolescents referred to mental health services. We used YSRs for referred adolescents in order to detect the syndromes that characterize individuals having severe enough problems to warrant referral. However, as described later in this chapter, norms for the problem scales were derived from the same nonreferred samples as were used to norm the competence scales.

The YSRs for referred adolescents were obtained in 1981-86 from 25 mental health services located mainly in the eastern United States, but including some as far west as Utah. The services included university child psychiatric clinics, community mental health centers, private practices, and inpatient services. To reflect sex differences in the patterning and prevalence of problems, separate analyses were performed for boys and girls. There were 486 boys and 441 girls having the SES and racial distributions shown in Table 2-2.

Table 2-2
Socioeconomic and Racial Distributions
of Referred Youth for Principal Components Analyses

	Boys N = 486	Girls N = 441	Combined[b] N = 927
SES[a]	%	%	%
Upper	17	19	18
Middle	23	20	22
Lower	27	21	24
Unknown	32	39	38
Mean	4.5	4.9	4.7
SD	2.6	2.5	2.6
Race			
White	71	67	69
Black	22	22	22
Mixed & Other	2	5	4
Unknown	5	6	6

Note. Because of rounding, columns may not sum to 100%.
[a] Hollingshead (1975) 9-step scale for parental occupation, using the higher status occupation where both parents were wage earners; scores 1-3.5 = Lower; 4-6.5 = Middle; 7-9 = Upper.
[b] Unweighted means of boys and girls.

Statistical Derivation of Syndromes

To identify items that were too rare or too common to contribute meaningfully to the statistical derivation of syndromes, we tabulated the percent of referred adolescents who endorsed each problem item (i.e., scored it 1 or 2). No item was endorsed by less than 5% or more than 95% of referred adolescents of either sex. All the problem items were therefore retained for analysis, except the open-ended item *56h. Other physical problems*, which covers diverse possibilities and has been omitted from our CBCL and TRF analyses. (The remainder of this section can be skipped by readers uninterested in the statistical derivation of syndromes.)

Separately for the referred boys and girls, we computed

Pearson correlations between all problem items except *56h*. The Pearson correlations were subjected to a principal components analysis, which is like a factor analysis, except that 1.0 is used instead of an estimated communality for each item. When over 100 items are used, as we did, principal components analyses produce results that are generally similar but somewhat superior to factor analyses using estimated item communalities (Gorsuch, 1983).

Orthogonal (varimax) rotations were performed on matrices ranging from 6 to 15 principal components in order to identify syndromes that remained relatively intact despite changes in the number of components. For both sexes, the rotation of 8 components was deemed to yield the best representation of the most robust factors. Six components were similar enough between the boys and girls to warrant the same names, as listed in Table 2-3. A seventh component, designated as *Self-Destructive/Identity Problems*, was found in a stable form for the boys, but did not have a clear counterpart among the girls.

For the retained components, the eigenvalues (sum of squared loadings) of the unrotated components ranged from 1.84 to 18.70, while for the rotated components they ranged from 3.34 to 9.76. All the components retained as bases for syndrome scales had at least 9 items that loaded ≥.30 (Appendix B lists the item loadings and eigenvalues for all the retained components).

Construction of Scales

Items with loadings ≥.30 on each of the retained components were used to construct problem scales for each sex. If an item loaded ≥.30 on more than one component, it was assigned to each of the scales for which it met this criterion. As a result, some items were assigned to two scales and a few were assigned to three. The association of some YSR problems with more than one syndrome is analogous to the association of certain physical symptoms, such as headache, with more than one illness.

As an example, we found that item *19. I try to get a lot of*

Table 2-3
Problem Scales Derived from the YSR

Group	Internalizing Scales[a]		Mixed	Externalizing Scales[b]	
Boys	Depressed	.84	Somatic Complaints	Aggressive	.86
	Unpopular	.81	Self-Destructive/ Identity Problems	Delinquent	.81
			Thought Disorder		
Girls	Somatic Complaints	.85	Unpopular	Delinquent	.90
	Depressed	.76	Thought Disorder	Aggressive	.81

[a] Scales are listed in descending order of the Internalizing loadings shown to the right of scale names and explained in Chapter 3.
[b] Scales are listed in descending order of the Externalizing loadings shown to the right of scale names and explained in Chapter 3.

attention loaded .41 on the *Aggressive* syndrome and .39 on the *Unpopular* syndrome for boys. Boys who report that they try to get a lot of attention *and* report many features of the Aggressive syndrome are apt to differ from those who report that they try to get a lot of attention *and* report many features of the Unpopular syndrome. Some boys may, of course, show many features of both syndromes, but the emergence of statistically distinct groupings indicates that they do not consistently occur together, despite having an item in common.

Comparison with CBCL and TRF Problem Scales

In our analyses of the CBCL and TRF (Achenbach & Edelbrock, 1983, 1986), as well as in analyses of the Dutch translation of the CBCL (Achenbach, Verhulst, Baron, & Althaus, 1987), the largest syndrome for all sex/age groups consisted of overtly aggressive behaviors similar to the syndrome designated as Aggressive in the YSR analyses. The Aggressive syndrome in the CBCL and TRF analyses had so many items with high loadings that only the items loading $\geq$.40 were retained for the problem scales.

Even though our analyses of the YSR yielded a syndrome for both sexes that included many of the same items as the CBCL and TRF Aggressive syndrome, the YSR syndrome did not account for as much variance or have so many high loading items as the CBCL and TRF Aggressive syndromes. Instead, the Depressed syndrome accounted for the most variance in the YSR self-ratings by both sexes. For girls, the eigenvalue of 9.76 for the rotated Depressed factor was considerably larger than that of the second largest factor, the Delinquent factor, which had an eigenvalue of 5.60. For boys, the Depressed factor's eigenvalue of 5.72 was also the largest, although it was not much larger than the second largest eigenvalue of 5.60 for the Delinquent factor.

The primacy of the Depressed factor in self-ratings but the Aggressive factor in parent and teacher ratings suggests an important difference in the problems that are most salient to adolescents versus their parents and teachers. Nevertheless, both the Depressed and Aggressive factors have clear counterparts in the ratings by all three types of rater, indicating that all their ratings reflect syndromal groupings of these problems. All the other YSR syndromes also have counterparts in parent and/or teacher ratings, except for the Self-Destructive/Identity Problems factor found in boys' YSR ratings.

Names for the Problem Scales

As done for the CBCL and TRF problem scales, we selected names for the YSR problem scales that are intended to summarize the content of each scale. The following scales were similar enough to scales scored from both the CBCL and TRF to warrant similar names: *Aggressive*, *Delinquent*, and *Depressed*. In addition, the *Somatic Complaints* scale has a clear counterpart scored from the CBCL, while the *Unpopular* scale has a clear counterpart scored from the TRF. The YSR *Thought Disorder* scale resembles the *Schizoid* scale scored from the CBCL, but differs enough to warrant a less nosological-sounding name.

It should be noted that the YSR Somatic Complaints scale for girls includes item *40. I hear things that nobody else seems able to hear (describe)* and *70. I see things that nobody else seems able to see (describe)*. These items are also included in the YSR Thought Disorder syndrome for both sexes, as well as the CBCL Schizoid syndrome. Although these items may suggest problems in reality testing, adolescents sometimes write descriptions such as "ringing in ears" or "spots before eyes." The association of items *40* and *70* with the YSR Somatic Complaints syndrome for girls is thus apt to reflect experiences like these, rather than poor reality testing. When items *40* and *70* are scored as present, it is always important to look at the respondent's descriptive comments, rather than automatically assuming that they indicate poor reality testing.

The YSR *Self-Destructive/Identity Problems* scale for boys has no clear counterparts in our analyses of the CBCL or TRF. The highest loading items were *18. I deliberately try to hurt or kill myself* (loading = .65); *91. I think about killing myself* (loading = .63); and *110. I wish I were of the opposite sex* (loading = .60). Because item *5. I act like the opposite sex* also had a moderate loading of .37 and most of the other items concern feelings of depression, worthlessness, being unloved, and jealousy, this syndrome involves distress likely to reflect concerns about sexual identity. Although the Self-Destructive syndrome found in TRF ratings of both sexes also included suicidal items *18* and *91*, it did not include problems of sexual identity or such a large proportion of dysphoric items. It therefore seems likely that assessment of the Self-Destructive/ Identity Problems syndrome depends more on self-reports than the syndromes that have clear counterparts in reports by parents and/or teachers. Conversely, the absence of counterparts to the hyperactive, inattentive, and withdrawal syndromes found in CBCL and/or TRF ratings suggests that assessment of these syndromes depends more on reports by others than self-reports.

Users are reminded that no scale is equivalent to a particular diagnosis. A high score on a particular scale, such as the Depressed scale, may be evidence in favor of a particular diagnosis, but multiple sources of data and the respondents' descriptive comments should be examined before drawing diagnostic conclusions. Detailed appraisals of relations between scale scores and diagnostic concepts are presented by Achenbach (1985), while Achenbach and McConaughy (1987) present practical applications of empirically-based assessment to diagnostic questions.

Scoring the Problem Scales

Case example. Figure 2-2 shows the behavior problem portion of the hand-scored YSR profile completed by Robert, the 15-year-old boy whose competence scales are shown in Figure 2-1. Each of the seven scales consists of items that were found to occur together in our analyses of self-ratings by 11- to 18-year-old boys referred for mental health services.

To compute Robert's score on each profile scale, the score (0, 1, or 2) that he circled for each item on the YSR is entered in the space beside the item on the YSR profile. (Appendix A provides detailed scoring instructions.) The scores for all the items of the scale are then summed to obtain the total raw score for that scale.

For example, on scale *I. Depressed*, Robert has scores of 1, 1, 2, 1, and 1 on items 9, 17, 35, 69, and 103, respectively. (Note that the items on the profile are abbreviated versions of those that are listed on the YSR.) We sum the 1, 1, 2, 1, and 1 to obtain Robert's total score of 6 for the Depressed scale. We then mark the interval that includes 6 in the column of numbers above the Depressed scale. Because 69% of boys in the normative sample obtained scores ranging from 0 to 12 on this scale,

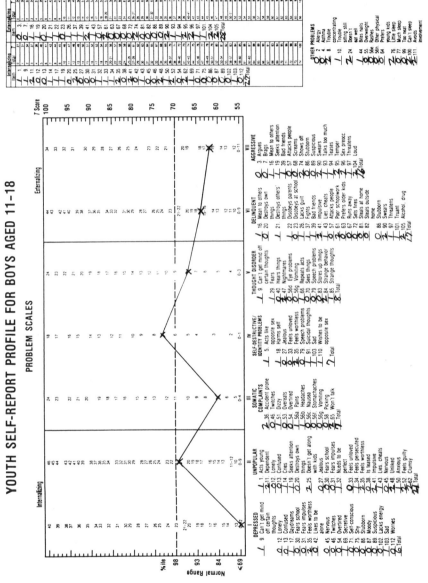

Fig 2-2. Problem scales of a hand-scored YSR profile completed for 15-year-old Robert.

the bottom interval—which includes 6—is marked. The percentiles at the left of the profile indicate the percent of boys in the normative sample who obtained scores less than or equal to each score. The T scores to the right of the profile can be used to provide a common numerical scale. To retain maximum differentiation among scores, the raw scale scores can be used for statistical analyses, if desired.

The other six scales are similarly scored by entering the 0, 1, or 2 that Robert circled for each item on the YSR and then summing them to obtain the total raw score for each scale. After all the raw scores have been marked in the graphic display, they can be connected to form a profile. The broken line across the profile at the 98th percentile ($T = 70$) indicates the border between the normal range and scores that are sufficiently deviant to be of concern because they exceed those of 98% of our normative sample. Figure 2-2 shows that Robert's score exceeded the 98th percentile on scale *IV. Self-Destructive/Identity Problems*, but that his other scores were in the normal range.

Assignment of Normalized T Scores to Raw Scores

(This section can be skipped by readers uninterested in the statistical details of standard scores.) As done for the CBCL and TRF profiles (Achenbach & Edelbrock, 1983, 1986), we computed the cumulative frequency distribution of total scores obtained on each scale by our normative samples of each sex. We then assigned normalized T scores to raw scores at each percentile, as specified by Abramowitz and Stegun (1968). However, for low scale scores and for scale scores above the 98th percentile, we departed from basing T scores strictly on percentiles in the following ways:

1. Low scores. As with most scales for problems, the distributions of scores on our problem scales are positively skewed. That is, many adolescents in the normative samples obtained low scores, while fewer obtained each successively higher score. Because the scales differ in the percent of adolescents obtaining the lowest possible raw score (i.e., 0), basing T scores exclusively on percentiles would cause big differences between the lowest possible T score on different scales.

The most extreme difference would be between the Depressed scale for girls, where 0.9% of the normative sample obtained a score of 0, and the Self-Destructive/Identity Problems scale for boys, where 33.1% obtained a score of 0. If T scores were based directly on percentiles, the lowest T score for the Depressed scale would be 26, whereas the lowest T score for the Self-Destructive/Identity Problems scale would be 46. Although a girl with a T score of 26 would seem to have a low score compared to a boy with a T score of 46, both would in fact have the lowest possible score on the respective scales—a raw score of 0, indicating that no problems were reported.

Another consideration is that, when every raw score increment is displayed on a profile, it is tempting to interpret all differences between scale scores as if they represented degrees of deviance. When the differences are all well within the normal range, this can be misleading, because a score at the 50th percentile is not more deviant than a score at the 40th percentile.

To equalize the starting points of the scales and to prevent overinterpretation of minor differences within the normal range, we assigned a T score of 55 to all raw scores at and below the 69th percentile of the cumulative frequency distribution obtained by our normative samples. As Figure 2-2 shows, all scales for boys have more than one raw score grouped at the bottom of the profile, equivalent to the 69th percentile and a T score of 55. On scale *I. Depressed*, for example, raw scores of 0 to 12 are all at the bottom of the profile. This merely means that 69% of the normative sample obtained scores of 12 or less and are given a T score of 55. (If a user wishes to preserve all the possible variance in scores, the raw scale scores can be used as an alternative to the T scores.)

2. High scores. Because most adolescents in the normative samples obtained relatively low raw scores, it was not possible to use percentiles as a basis for assigning T scores to the raw scores at the high end of each scale. On the Self-Destructive/Identity Problems scale for boys, for example, the maximum possible score is 18, but 98% of the normative sample obtained scores of 6 or less. Furthermore, above the 98th percentile, most of the scores were not obtained by any adolescents in the normative sample. Basing T scores on percentiles above the 98th percentile would thus not really reflect reliable aspects of the distribution of scores obtained by non-referred adolescents.

We therefore based T scores on percentiles only up to the 98th percentile of the raw scale scores. For the scale scores above the 98th percentile ($T = 70$), we assigned T scores from 71 to 100 in as many increments as there were raw scores on a scale. For example, on the Self-Destructive/Identity Problems scale, the raw score at the 98th percentile was 6, which was assigned a T score of 70. Because there are 9 items on the scale, the maximum possible score is 18 (i.e., if a boy circled a score of 2 on all 9 items, his total raw score would be 18). There are 30 intervals from 71 to 100, but only 12 raw scores from 7 through 18. To assign T scores to the 12 raw scores, we divided 30 by 12. Because $30/12 = 2.5$, T scores were assigned to raw scores in intervals of 2.5. Thus, a raw score of 7 was assigned a T score of $70 + 2.5 = 72.5$, rounded off to 73. A raw score of 8 was assigned a T score of $72.5 + 2.5 = 75$, and so on. A look at the relations between raw scores and T scores above 70 in Figure 2-2 should help to make this clear.

PROBLEMS OMITTED FROM SCALES OF THE PROFILE

For each sex, some items did not have loadings that met the criterion of .30 on any of the rotated components used to construct problem scales. These items were therefore not included in problem scales for that sex. This does not mean, however, that such items are not important. It means only that they did not help to *discriminate* statistically among the empirically-derived syndromes. Such items are listed under the heading *Other Problems* on the profile, as shown in Figure 2-2. Although these items are not scored on the problem scales for that sex, they are counted toward the adolescent's total problem score, as described next.

TOTAL PROBLEM SCORE

The total problem score is the sum of 1s and 2s circled by the adolescent on all the problem items. There are 102 problem items, plus space to write in additional physical problems (item *56h*). As specified in the scoring instructions (Appendix A), one physical problem written in by the adolescent can be counted toward the total problem score. If the adolescent has written in and scored more than one additional physical problem, the one receiving the highest score is included in the total problem score. For example, if two additional problems were written in for item *56h*, and they were both scored 1, only a score of 1 would be added to the total problem score. On the other hand, if either of the additional physical problems were scored 2, a score of 2 would be added to the total problem score. The total problem score can thus range from 0 (if an adolescent circles 0 for every item) to 206 (if an adolescent circles 2 on all 102 problem items, plus 2 for at least one additional physical problem on item *56h*). Adding a maximum of 2 points for item *56h* is intended to limit the variance contributed by items that are not stated for other adolescents to rate.

Normalized T Scores

We assigned normalized T scores to the total problem scores in much the same way as to the problem scales, with two differences:

1. The total number of items is much greater than the number on any problem scale, and most adolescents report at least some of them. Consequently, few adolescents in our normative samples obtained extremely low total problem scores. It therefore seemed unnecessary to set a minimum T score at which to group low raw scores as we did for the problem scales. Instead, we based normalized T scores directly on the percentiles of the distribution of total scores obtained by our normative samples, up to the 98th percentile ($T = 70$).

2. No adolescent in either our normative or referred samples obtained anywhere near the highest possible raw score of 206. If we had assigned T scores above the 98th percentile by dividing all the top raw scores into the 30 intervals from 71 to 100, we would have compressed scores actually obtained by our referred samples into a narrow range of T scores. We would also have assigned raw scores above those actually obtained to a broad range of T scores. For example, the highest total score obtained in our sample of referred girls was 151. If we had assigned equal T score intervals to the raw scores from the 98th percentile (raw score $= 90$) to the highest possible raw score (206), only 17 T scores would have been allocated to the 61 raw scores that we actually found, whereas 13 T scores would have been allocated to the 45 raw scores above those actually found.

    To allow the upper T scores to reflect differences among raw scores actually apt to occur, we assigned a T score of 89 to the highest raw score found in our referred sample for each sex. The raw scores from the 98th percentile to the highest raw score were then assigned T scores in equal intervals from 71 to 89. The raw scores above the highest actually found in our referred sample were assigned T scores in equal intervals from 90 through 100. (Appendix A lists the T score assigned to each total raw score for each sex.)

Missing Data

As indicated in the scoring instructions (Appendix A), the problem portion of the profile should *not* be scored if data are missing for more than 8 problem items, not counting item *56h*, unless it is clear that the adolescent intended omitted items to be scored 0.

SUMMARY

The Youth Self-Report Profile is designed to compare an adolescent's self-ratings with those obtained from normative groups of adolescents. Hand-scoring forms and computer programs are available for scoring the profile. Scores for involvement in activities, social relationships, academic performance, and the sum of these are entered on the competence portion of the profile, which indicates percentiles and normalized T scores based on normative samples of nonreferred adolescents of each sex. The normative samples comprised 686 randomly-selected adolescents living in the Worcester, Massachusetts, metropolitan area.

Problem scales were constructed from principal components analyses of YSRs completed by 927 adolescents referred for mental health services. Analyses were done separately for each sex. Percentiles and normalized T scores were derived from the scores obtained by adolescents in the normative sample of each sex. All scores up to the 69th percentile in the normative samples were assigned a T score of 55. T scores from 55 to 70 were based on the 69th to the 98th percentiles of the normative samples. T scores from 71 to 100 were assigned in increments corresponding to the remaining raw scores of each scale.

For the total problem score, normalized T scores were based entirely on percentiles up to a T score of 70 (98th percentile). We then assigned T scores from 71 to 89 to raw scores in increments ranging from the 98th percentile of the normative sample to the highest score obtained in the clinical sample of each sex. The remaining possible raw scores, up to a maximum of 206, were assigned T scores in intervals from 90 to 100.

Chapter 3
The Internalizing-Externalizing Dichotomy

Although our analyses showed that six syndromes could be identified from YSR ratings by girls and seven from ratings by boys, much of the clinical literature focuses on two broad-band groupings of child and adolescent problems. These groupings have been repeatedly identified in other multivariate analyses (for reviews, see Achenbach, 1985; Achenbach & Edelbrock, 1978; Quay, 1986). They reflect a distinction between inhibited, overcontrolled behavior, and aggressive, antisocial, undercontrolled behavior. They have been designated with such terms as Personality Problem versus Conduct Problem (Peterson, 1961); Inhibition versus Aggression (Miller, 1967); Internalizing versus Externalizing (Achenbach, 1966); and Overcontrolled versus Undercontrolled (Achenbach & Edelbrock, 1978).

DERIVING BROAD-BAND GROUPINGS

Because broad-band groupings of problems may be useful for certain purposes, we performed second-order principal components analyses of our narrow-band problem scales. We did this as follows:

1. Within the clinical samples on which we did our first-order principal components analyses, we computed each adolescent's raw score on the six or seven problem scales for that sex.

2. We then converted each adolescent's raw scores to the normalized T scores that had been derived from the normative samples (described in Chapter 2). Because some items were scored on more than one problem scale, we counted these items only on the scale that they loaded highest on for each sex.

3. We computed Pearson correlations between the T scores on the problem scales for each sex.

4. We performed principal components analyses of the inter-correlations among the problem scales.

5. We performed varimax rotations of the second-order principal components.

For both sexes, the first two second-order components corresponded to the dichotomy between overcontrolled and undercontrolled problems found in other studies. The exact composition of the two second-order components differed between the sexes, owing to differences in the composition of the narrow-band scales from which they were derived and differences in the alignment of the narrow-band scales on the second-order components. However, they were similar enough to the Internalizing-Externalizing dichotomy found previously (Achenbach, 1966; Achenbach & Edelbrock, 1983, 1986) to be given the same names. Table 2-3 (Chapter 2) shows the loadings of the narrow-band scales on the second-order Internalizing and Externalizing components.

On the YSR profile, the narrow-band scales are arranged in the order of their loadings on the second-order components: Starting at the left of the profile, the scale having the highest loading on the Internalizing component is followed by the other one that had a high loading on the Internalizing component. Then come scales that did not have high loadings on either of the two components. These scales are followed by the scale having the second highest loading on the Externalizing component. The profile ends on the right with the scale having the highest loading on the Externalizing component.

NORMING THE INTERNALIZING AND EXTERNALIZING GROUPINGS

To provide norm-referenced scores for Internalizing and Externalizing, we summed the scores obtained by members of the normative sample of each sex on all the Internalizing items and all the Externalizing items. Items belonging to more than one Internalizing scale were counted only once in the Internalizing score, while items belonging to more than one Externalizing scale were counted only once in the Externalizing score. However, items belonging to both an Internalizing and an Externalizing scale were each counted once in both the Internalizing and Externalizing scores.

Assigning Normalized T Scores

Separately for each sex, the distributions of total raw scores for Internalizing and Externalizing were used to derive normalized T scores in the same way as for the total problem scores, as explained in Chapter 2. To assess an adolescent's problems in terms of the broad-band Internalizing—Externalizing distinction, the hand-scored YSR profile provides a table for entering and summing all the Internalizing items and all the Externalizing items. The table also indicates the T score assigned to each total raw score for Internalizing and Externalizing (see Appendix A for detailed scoring instructions). The computer-scored version of the profile automatically provides the adolescent's total raw scores and T scores for Internalizing and Externalizing.

RELATIONS BETWEEN INTERNALIZING AND EXTERNALIZING SCORES

Although the Internalizing and Externalizing groupings reflect contrasting types of problems, they are not mutually exclusive. The degree and direction of correlation between them depends on characteristics of the sample studied. The average of the Pearson correlations between total Internalizing and total Externalizing T scores was .55 in the clinical samples of each sex from which the scales were derived. Across our two normative samples, the average correlation was .54. (In computing these correlations, we deleted the few items that are scored on both an Internalizing scale and an Externalizing scale, but Appendix D presents the correlations for both sexes without deletion of redundant items.)

Even without the few overlapping items, there is clearly a positive association between problems that have often been viewed as opposites. This is because there is a general dimension among problems that resembles the general *(g)* dimension among ability tests: Individuals who obtain very high scores in one area tend to be above average in other areas, whereas individuals who obtain very low scores in one area tend to be below average in other areas as well.

Despite the positive association between Internalizing and Externalizing found in our samples as a whole, however, some adolescents' problems are primarily Internalizing, whereas other adolescents' problems are primarily Externalizing. This is analogous to the relation between Verbal IQ and Performance IQ on the Wechsler intelligence tests: Across groups, there is a positive correlation between the Verbal and Performance IQ, but some individuals have much lower scores in one area than the other. For these individuals, different scores in different areas form a pattern that distinguishes them from those whose scores show the opposite pattern. Similarly, classification of Internalizers versus Externalizers may be meaningful only for those who show relatively extreme discrepancies between these two broad-band scores.

Distinguishing between Internalizers and Externalizers

How large a difference between scores is required to mark an adolescent's self-report as indicating a primarily Internalizing versus Externalizing pattern? This depends on the user's purpose. The stringency of criteria for classifying adolescents as Internalizers versus Externalizers will affect the proportion of a sample classified, the homogeneity of the resulting groups, and the strength of the association between the Internalizing-Externalizing dichotomy and other variables. Very stringent criteria, for example, will severely limit the proportion of adolescents classified as Internalizers or Externalizers. But stringent criteria will also produce relatively pure groups of Internalizers and Externalizers who are likely to differ more on other variables than would less pure Internalizing and Externalizing groups.

The trade-offs between stringency of criteria, proportion of adolescents classified, and degree of association with other variables must be judged by users of the YSR in light of their own purposes. We suggest, however, that adolescents not be classified as Internalizers or Externalizers unless *(a)* their total problem score exceeds the 89th percentile for their sex, *and (b)* there is a difference of at least 10 points between their Internalizing and Externalizing T score. Requiring the total score to exceed the 89th percentile ensures that the adolescents have reported enough problems to be in the clinical range (raw score >68 for boys; >70 for girls). Otherwise the discrepancy between Internalizing and Externalizing scores may be based on too few items to be meaningful. The larger the difference between T scores, the "purer" the Internalizing and Externalizing groups will be.

SUMMARY

Second-order principal components analyses of the YSR problem scales showed that the scales form two broad-band groupings for both sexes. These groupings correspond to the distinction between inhibited, overcontrolled problems versus aggressive, antisocial, undercontrolled problems that has long been familiar to those who work with children and youth. We call these groupings *Internalizing* and *Externalizing*, respectively. On the YSR profile for each sex, the narrow-band problem scales are arranged according to their loadings on the second-order components. Starting at the left of the profile, the scale with the highest loading on the Internalizing component is followed by those with lower loadings on the Internalizing component and then those with progressively higher loadings on the Externalizing component, ending on the right with the scale having the highest loading on the Externalizing component. Two scales for girls and three scales for boys were not clearly aligned with either the Internalizing or Externalizing component and are not counted as part of either one. T scores for Internalizing and Externalizing are derived from the same normative samples as the T scores for the narrow-band problem scales.

Like Verbal IQ and Performance IQ on ability tests, the Internalizing and Externalizing scores are positively correlated with each other across entire samples of adolescents. However, some adolescents have much higher scores on one broad-band grouping than the other. The stringency of criteria for classifying adolescents as Internalizers or Externalizers should be based on the user's objectives. We suggest that adolescents not be classified as Internalizers or Externalizers unless their total problem score exceeds the 89th percentile for their sex *and* there is a difference of at least 10 points between their Internalizing and Externalizing *T* scores.

Chapter 4
Test-Retest Reliability and Stability

Because the YSR is designed to obtain adolescents' self-reports about their own functioning, the main way to assess reliability is to compare YSR responses on two occasions across an interval long enough to avoid much recall but short enough to avoid major changes in the target phenomena. We assessed reliability by asking 50 adolescents in our normative sample to complete the YSR twice at intervals averaging 7 days. We analyzed the relations between Time 1 and Time 2 scores in two ways: *(a)* Pearson correlations, symbolized by *r*, which mainly reflect similarities in *rank ordering* between the two sets of scores; and *(b)* *t* tests, which mainly reflect differences between the *mean magnitudes* of the two sets of scores.

Because Pearson *r* reflects similarities between the rank orders of scores at Time 1 and Time 2, it is high if self-ratings by individual adolescents retain approximately the same rank compared to those of other adolescents in the sample. Because it is not determined by the absolute magnitude of scores, *r* can be high even if all the Time 1 scores differ in magnitude from all the Time 2 scores. The *t* test, by contrast, indicates the magnitude of the difference between the sets of scores relative to their variance. A *t* test could therefore show that there is no significant difference between Time 1 and Time 2 scores, even though a low *r* indicates that individuals have changed their ranks from Time 1 to Time 2. By reporting both the *r* and the results of the *t* test for Time 1 versus Time 2 scores, we enable the reader to consider consistency separately for rank order and for the magnitude of scores.

Table 4-1 presents the 1-week test-retest *r* for raw scores on each scale computed separately for boys and girls. It also presents Pearson *r*s for *T* scores for both sexes combined for all scales except Self-Destructive/Identity Problems—which exists only for boys—and for mean School Performance—which is scored as a single item with no *T* scores. The median of the 39 *r*s in Table 4-1 is .81.

Table 4-1
One-Week Test-Retest Reliabilities

	Boys N=22	Girls N=28	Both Sexes N=50
Competence Scales			
Activities	.68	.84	.67
Social	.80	.79	.75[ab]
School	.83	.87	—
Total Competence	.80	.83	.83
Problem Scales			
Aggressive	.82[ab]	.85[a]	.62
Delinquent	.77	.94	.63
Depressed	.84	.88[ab]	.81
Self-Destructive/			
Identity Problems	.68	—	—
Somatic Complaints	.81	.44[ab]	.56
Thought Disorder	(.33)	.85	.39
Unpopular	.70	.59[ab]	.51
Internalizing	.81	.86[a]	.83[ab]
Externalizing	.79	.92[a]	.87[a]
Total Problems	.78	.86[a]	.86[a]

Note. Table entries are Pearson correlations between YSR ratings at a mean interval of 7 days. For each sex, correlations are for raw scores. For both sexes combined, correlations are for T scores on scales that are similar for both sexes. All correlations are significant at $p<.05$ except the one in parentheses. Median r for entire table = .81. Mean difference between Time 1 and Time 2 scores = 1.2.
[a] Time 1 > Time 2, $p<.05$ by t test.
[b] When corrected for number of comparisons, Time 1 vs. Time 2 difference is not significant.

Most of the scale scores declined somewhat from Time 1 to Time 2, a phenomenon that has been repeatedly found for many rating scales (Achenbach & Edelbrock, 1983, 1986; Evans, 1975; Milich et al., 1980; Miller et al., 1972). Similar declines in reported problems have also been found in psychiatric interviews of children and adolescents—such as the Diagnostic Interview Schedule for Children (DISC; Edelbrock et al., 1985), as well as in interviews of adults (Robins, 1985). The superscript *a* in Table 4-1 indicates the 12 comparisons in which the decline in scores was statistically significant at $p<.05$ by *t* test. At least 6 out of 39 comparisons could be significant by chance using a $p<.01$ protection level (Feild & Armenakis, 1974; Sakoda, Cohen, & Beall, 1954). We have therefore marked with superscript *b* the 6 $p<.05$ differences that are the most likely due to chance because they had the smallest *t* values.

The magnitude of changes in scores was generally small, with the mean difference between Time 1 and Time 2 scores being 1.2 points. The largest difference was on the total problem raw score for girls, where the mean dropped 7.3 points, from 37.2 to 29.9 on a scale ranging from 0 to 206. The next largest drops were 3.4 for the girls' Internalizing raw score and 3.2 for the total problem *T* score for girls and boys combined. Both these scores are, of course, closely related to the girls' total problem raw score.

AGE DIFFERENCES

Because age differences have been found in the test-retest reliability of structured interviews with adolescents, such as the DISC (Edelbrock et al., 1985), we compared the correlations for 11- to 14-year-olds with those for 15- to 18-year-olds. Test-retest correlations were computed on raw scores for each sex separately and on *T* scores with the sexes combined. The relatively small samples of each sex in each age range limits the value of comparing correlations scale by scale. However, the median *r* of .77 for 11- to 14-year-olds versus .89 for 15- to 18-year-olds does indicate a general tendency for reliability to be better among the older adolescents. The median *r* of .89 is similar to the median 1-week test-retest reliability of .89 found for parents' ratings on the CBCL and .90 for teachers' ratings on the TRF (Achenbach & Edelbrock, 1983, 1986). YSR ratings by 15- to 18-year-olds are thus as reliable as parent and teacher ratings, while YSR ratings by 11- to 14-year-olds are not quite as reliable. A similar age trend was found by Edelbrock et al. (1985) for DISC interviews, where test-retest intraclass correlations averaged .60 for 10- to 13-year-olds and .71 for 14- to 18-year-olds.

SIX-MONTH STABILITY OF
CBCL SELF-RATINGS

Prior to developing the YSR, we obtained test-retest self-ratings from referred 12- to 17-year-olds who filled out the behavior problem portion of the CBCL at intake into a community mental health center and again at a 6-month follow-up. Despite the third-person wording of the items, the inclusion of 16 CBCL items deemed inappropriate for the YSR, and the mental health services received in the interim, the r between total problem scores across the 6-month interval was .69 ($p<.001$, $N = 30$). As summarized in Table 4-2, this exceeded the test-retest r of .59 for mothers' ratings and .53 for a clinician's ratings across the same 6-month period. Table 4-2 also shows significant concurrent correlations between the adolescents, their mothers, and the clinician at intake and the 6-month follow-up. (The clinician's ratings were not entirely independent of the self-ratings and mothers' ratings, because the clinician had access to both these sets of ratings, as well as teacher ratings, family history, and interviews with the adolescents and their parents.)

Table 4-2
Correlations between CBCL Total Problem Scores from
Ratings by Referred Youth, their Mothers, and a Clinician

| | Intake | | 6-Month Follow-up | | |
Intake	Clinician	Mother	Clinician	Mother	Youth
Clinician			.53	.49	.40
Mother	.70		.38	.59	(.13)
Youth	.55	.37	(.14)	.44	.69
6-Month Follow-up					
Mother			.62		
Youth			.48	.56	

Note: *Ns* range from 27 for Intake Youth x Follow-up Clinician to 73 for Intake Mother x Intake Clinician. Table is from Achenbach & Edelbrock, 1983. All *rs* are significant at $p<.05$ except those in parentheses.

EIGHT-MONTH STABILITY OF YSR RATINGS

Table 4-3 presents Pearson rs for YSR ratings by a general population sample of 12- to 14-year-old students who completed the YSR on two occasions at intervals averaging about 8 months. All but the Self-Destructive/Identity Probems scale showed significant stability in rank ordering of scores. The median of the 39 rs in Table 4-3 is .51. The correlations tended to be somewhat higher for girls whose mean $r = .65$, than for boys whose mean $r = .46$ (computed by z transformation for the 13 scales common to both sexes). A similar but smaller tendency was evident in the 1-week test-retest correlations, where the mean $r = .84$ for girls and .77 for boys. As is evident from Table 4-3, the correlations for the T scores of both sexes combined on some scales were considerably lower than for the raw scores for either sex. This reflects the small amount of variance for the T scores on those scales for nonreferred adolescents. It is especially evident on the Aggressive scale, where most of the subjects obtained the minimum possible T score of 55 and the mean was only 57.

Table 4-3
Eight-Month Test-Retest Stabilities

	Boys	Girls	Both Sexes
Competence Scales	N = 48	54	102
Activities	.40[ac]	.35[bc]	.31
Social	.57	.49	.46
School	.61	.57	—
Total Competence	.69	.48	.61
Problem Scales			
Aggressive	.51	.64	.28
Delinquent	.44	.70	.34
Depressed	.37	.77	.33
Self-Destructive/Identity Problems	(.28)	—	—
Somatic Complaints	.29	.62	.44
Thought Disorder	.38	.61	.42
Unpopular	.41	.68	.45

Table 4-3 (Cont'd)

	Boys	Girls	Both Sexes
Internalizing	.40	.78	.65
Externalizing	.48	.70	.64
Total Problems	.43	.78	.67

Note. From B.E. Compas, D.C. Howell, V.S. Phares, & R. Williams, unpublished data. Table entries are Pearson correlations between YSR ratings at a mean interval of 8 months. For each sex, correlations are for raw scores. For both sexes combined, correlations are for *T* scores on scales that are similar for both sexes. All correlations are significant at $p < .05$ except the one in parentheses. Median *r* for entire table = .51. Mean differences between Time 1 and Time 2 scores = 0.4.
[a]Time 1 > Time 2, $p < .05$ by *t* test.
[b]Time 2 > Time 1, $p < .05$ by *t* test.
[c]When corrected for number of comparisons, Time 1 vs. Time 2 difference is not significant.

Among the 39 *t* test comparisons of Time 1 versus Time 2 scores, 2 showed a significant ($p < .05$) change in mean scores. This is less than expected by chance in 39 comparisons. The mean difference between Time 1 and Time 2 scores across all 39 comparisons was only 0.4 points.

SUMMARY

For raw scores on all YSR scales computed separately for each sex and *T* scores for the sexes combined, the median 1-week test-retest *r* was .81 for 50 nonreferred adolescents. There was a tendency for most scores to decline slightly over the 1-week interval, with the mean change across all scales being 1.2 points. The median 1-week test-retest *r* was .77 for 11- to 14-year-olds and .89 for 15- to 18-year-olds, which is similar to the test-retest reliability for parents' CBCL ratings and teachers' TRF ratings. Self-ratings by clinically-referred adolescents on the CBCL showed a test-retest *r* of .69 for total problem scores over a 6-month period. Self-ratings by nonreferred adolescents showed a median test-retest *r* of .51 and an *r* of .67 for total problems over an 8-month period, with a mean change of 0.4 across all scales.

Chapter 5
Validity

Validity concerns the accuracy with which a procedure measures what it is supposed to measure. The YSR is designed to obtain adolescents' reports of their own problems and competencies in a standardized format. Like other procedures for assessing behavioral/emotional problems and competencies, the validity of the YSR must be evaluated in relation to a variety of criteria, none of which is definitive by itself.

Our manuals for the CBCL and TRF (Achenbach & Edelbrock, 1983, 1986) provided evidence of construct validity for CBCL and TRF syndromes in terms of significant correlations with syndrome scales derived from other instruments. However, the lack of instruments resembling the YSR currently limits the possibilities for testing construct validity in this way. It is our hope that the availability of the YSR will encourage further work on syndromes identified via adolescent self-reports as one avenue for testing construct validity. In the meantime, Chapter 7 presents correlations between YSR and CBCL scale scores. The different perspectives of adolescents and their parents, however, limit the potential for testing construct validity via correlations of this sort. In this chapter, we will present findings on the content validity of YSR items and the criterion-related validity of the YSR scales.

CONTENT VALIDITY OF YSR ITEMS

Content validity refers to whether an instrument's content includes what it is intended to measure. The YSR items are based on CBCL items that were developed to describe competencies and problems that are of concern to parents and mental health workers. The CBCL items were derived from earlier research on child/adolescent psychiatric case histories (Achenbach, 1966), the clinical and research literature, and consultation with clinical and developmental psychologists, psychiatrists, and social workers. Pilot editions of the CBCL were tested with parents in several clinics and were revised on the basis of feedback from parents, paraprofessionals, and clinicians.

After finalizing the items, we compared CBCL item scores obtained by clinically referred and nonreferred children and adolescents ($N = 1300$ in each sample). On all but two of the CBCL problem items (*Allergy* and *Asthma*), the referred sample obtained significantly ($p < .005$) higher scores than the nonreferred sample. Except for *Allergy* and *Asthma*, the CBCL problem items were thus significantly associated with referrals for mental health services that had been made on grounds other than the CBCL.

As shown in Figures 1-1 and 1-2, 17 competence items and 102 problem items, plus an open-ended item for other physical problems, were adapted to the YSR from the CBCL. The CBCL items deemed inappropriate for the YSR included three competence items concerning special class placement, grade repetition, and other school problems, plus 16 problem items, such as CBCL item *6. Bowel movements outside toilet* and *98. Thumb-sucking*, which are at too young a level or are seldom acknowledged by adolescents. The 16 omitted problem items were replaced with socially desirable items that encourage respondents to report something favorable about themselves.

To test the associations between adolescents' YSR responses and referral for mental health services, we compared the scores obtained on every item by 715 adolescents referred for mental health services and 779 demographically similar nonreferred adolescents drawn from the normative sample described in Chapter 2. We sought to form samples that included 50 referred and 50 nonreferred adolescents of each sex at each age from 11 to 18. The samples fell short of our goal of 400 referred and 400 nonreferred of each sex, however, owing to the difficulty of reaching enough 17- and 18-year-olds either through home visits or child/adolescent mental health services. The samples totaled 366 referred boys, 388 nonreferred boys, 349 referred girls, and 391 nonreferred girls. (Chapter 6 reports sample sizes by 2-year age levels, referral status, and sex.)

The referred and nonreferred samples were matched as closely as possible for SES and race (blacks and whites only, since there were too few of other races to analyze separately). On Hollingshead's (1975) 9-step scale for parental occupation, the mean SES was 5.0 (SD = 2.4) for both the referred and nonreferred samples. Racial distributions were 17% black and 83% white for both samples.

As detailed in Chapter 6, the referred adolescents scored themselves significantly higher ($p < .01$) on 89 of the 102 specific problem items. This is a somewhat smaller proportion of problem items than found to show significant differences between referred and nonreferred samples in parents' CBCL ratings (116 out of 118 items; Achenbach & Edelbrock, 1981) and teachers' TRF ratings (117 out of 118 items; Achenbach & Edelbrock, 1986). Nevertheless, it indicates that self-ratings on most of the YSR problem items are significantly related to mental health concerns.

As detailed in Chapter 6, referred adolescents scored lower than nonreferred adolescents on 10 of the 17 competence items, but higher on 2 of the 17, including number of sports and number of nonsports recreational activities. Because all the competence items yielded higher scores for nonreferred than referred samples in parents' CBCL ratings (Achenbach & Edelbrock, 1981), they are validly related to mental health concerns when reported by parents, but less consistently so when reported by adolescents. (The competence items are replaced with school-related adaptive functioning items on the TRF.)

As discussed further in Chapter 6, there is evidence from other research that disturbed youngsters tend to rate themselves more favorably than normal youngsters (Zimet & Farley, 1987) and more favorably than adults rate them (Kazdin, French, & Unis, 1983; Piers, 1972; Zimet & Farley, 1986).

Although parent, teacher, and self-report versions of nearly all the YSR problem items thus have significant associations with referral for mental health services, the self-report versions of the competence items showed less consistent associations. Self-reports of some of the competence items may be more useful as indices of self-perceptions than of actual competencies, but prospective users should judge for themselves whether the content of the YSR items suits their purposes.

CRITERION-RELATED VALIDITY
OF YSR SCALES

One of the main reasons for our empirical derivation of syndromes was the lack of a satisfactory taxonomy of child and adolescent disorders. Although efforts have been made to increase the precision of diagnostic criteria (American Psychiatric Association, 1980, 1987), the diagnostic categories have not been derived from assessment of children and adolescents. As discussed in Chapter 8 and presented in more detail elsewhere (Achenbach, 1985; Achenbach & McConaughy, 1987; Edelbrock, 1984), there are similarities and statistical associations between several diagnostic categories and our empirically-derived syndromes. Nevertheless, the existing diagnostic categories have not been adequately validated, nor are they operationally defined according to any particular assessment procedures. We have therefore used as a validity criterion actual referral for mental health services in order to test the criterion-related validity of the CBCL and TRF problem scales.

We recognize that referral for mental health services is not an infallible criterion of adolescents' need for help. Some adolescents in our referred sample may not really have needed professional help, whereas some in our nonreferred sample may have needed help. Yet, as detailed elsewhere (Achenbach & Edelbrock, 1981), actual referral seemed as ecologically valid as any other practical alternative for large samples.

Using YSRs for the 715 referred and 779 nonreferred adolescents described earlier, we did separate analyses for the 754 boys and 740 girls from these samples. To assess the effects of referral status and the demographic variables, we computed partial correlations of each problem scale with referral status (scored 1 for nonreferred, 2 for referred), age, SES (Hollingshead 9-step scale), and race (scored 1 for white, 2 for black). Each partial correlation assessed the association between a scale score and either referral status, age, SES, or race, with the other three partialled out.

The results are displayed in Table 5-1. In view of our large sample sizes, many analyses, and numerous significant effects, we accepted as significant only those effects that were significant at $p < .01$. Two effects in each Table 5-1 column of 14 analyses for boys and 13 analyses for girls could reach the $p < .01$ level of significance by chance, using a .01 protection level (Sakoda, Cohen, & Beall, 1954). To indicate the effects most likely to be chance, we have marked with a superscript d the two smallest significant effects in each column.

Table 5-1
Percent of Variance Accounted for by Significant ($p < .01$)
Effects of Referral Status, Age, Race, and
SES in Partial Correlations

	Boys $N = 754$			Girls $N = 740$		
	Ref. Stat.[a]	Age[b]	SES[c]	Ref. Stat.[a]	Age[b]	SES[c]
Competence Scales						
Activities	—	1^{dY}	$<1^U$	2^{dR}	2^Y	1^U
Social	6^N	—	2^U	4^{dN}	$<1^{dY}$	—
School	7^N	—	2^U	8^N	—	—
Total Competence	2^{dN}	1^Y	2^U	—	—	—
Problem Scales						
Aggressive	4^{dR}	—	—	8^R	3°	1^L
Delinquent	9^R	—	1^L	10^R	2^O	1^{dL}
Depressed	9^R	—	—	13^R	2^O	—
Self-Destructive/ Identity Problems	5^R	—	—	Not scored for girls		
Somatic Complaints	5^R	4^Y	—	9^R	—	2^L
Thought Disorder	11^R	1^{dY}	$<1^{dL}$	19^R	—	1^L
Unpopular	9^R	1^Y	—	8^R	1^Y	1^{dL}
Internalizing	10^R	—	—	13^R	1^O	—
Externalizing	7^R	—	$<1^{dL}$	11^R	3°	1^L
Total Problems	11^R	—	—	14^R	$<1^{dO}$	1^L

Note. Percent of variance is shown for effects significant at $p < .01$.
Effects of race are not listed, because only one very small effect was significant for each sex, which is less than expected by chance.
[a]N = higher scores for nonreferred youth; R = higher scores for referred youth.
[b]O = higher scores for older youth; Y = higher scores for younger youth.
[c]L = higher scores for lower SES; U = higher scores for upper SES.
[d]Not significant when corrected for number of analyses.

To summarize the magnitude of the significant effects for comparison with each other and with our findings for the CBCL and TRF scales, Table 5-1 lists the percent of variance accounted for by each effect that was significant at $p < .01$. The percent of variance was computed by squaring the partial correlation coefficient for each effect. The first entry in Table 5-1, for example, indicates that the Activities scale showed no significant effect of referral status for boys, a 1% effect of age, and a <1% effect of SES. According to Cohen's (1977) criteria for partial correlations, effects accounting for 2 to 13% of the variance are small; 13-26% are medium; and ≥26% are large.

(In our CBCL and TRF analyses, we accomplished the same objectives by using partial regression coefficients. In those analyses, we used $p < .05$ as our criterion for significance, because the division of samples by age, as well as by sex, resulted in smaller Ns than in the YSR analyses.)

Effects of Demographic Variables

Racial effects are not listed in Table 5-1, because only one was significant for each sex, these were less than expected by chance, and neither of them accounted for more than 1% of variance. The racial effects indicated a slight tendency for black boys to score higher than white boys on the Thought Disorder scale (<1% of variance) and white girls to score higher than black girls on school performance (1% of variance).

Age effects were evident in 5 of the 14 analyses for boys, with younger boys scoring higher on the Activities, total competence, Somatic Complaints, Thought Disorder, and Unpopular scales. The only age effect exceeding 1% of the variance for boys was on the Somatic Complaints scale, where the 4% accounted for by age meets Cohen's criteria for a small effect. Significant age effects were evident in 9 of the 13 analyses for girls, with younger girls obtaining higher scores on 2 competence scales and lower scores on 6 of the 7 problem scales that showed significant age effects. The largest age effects for girls accounted for 3% of the variance on the Aggressive and Externalizing scales.

SES effects were similar to those found in parent and teacher ratings (Achenbach & Edelbrock, 1983, 1986), in that they reflected higher competence scores and lower problem scores for upper SES adolescents. None of the SES effects exceeded 2% of the variance on the YSR scales, however.

Effects of Referral Status

Referral status had significant effects on all scores, except Activities for boys and total competence for girls. All the significant effects reflected lower competence and higher problem scores for referred adolescents, except for the Activities scale for girls. Nearly all the effects of referral status were considerably larger than the demographic effects on the same scales. (Appendix C presents means, standard deviations, and standard errors for all scale scores.)

Competence Scales. Among the competence scores, neither the Activities scale nor the total competence score (of which the Activities scale is a large component) appear to be effective discriminators between referred and nonreferred groups. The score for school performance discriminated better than the other competence scores, with referral status accounting for 7% of the variance for boys and 8% for girls. However, it is not applicable to adolescents who are not in school. On the Social scale, referral status accounted for 6% of variance for boys and 4% for girls, but the differences between the distributions of scores for referred and nonreferred adolescents were not large enough to offer much discriminative power. In light of these findings, we conclude that the competence scores may be useful in describing particular strengths and weaknesses acknowledged by individual adolescents, but not in determining clinical status. For the remainder of this chapter, we will therefore focus on the validity of the problem scores.

Problem Scales. Medium effects of referral status were found on three scales, all of them for girls, including Thought Disorder (19%), Internalizing (13.2%), and total problems (14%). The Depressed scale for girls fell just below Cohen's criterion for medium effects, accounting for 12.7% of variance, rounded to 13% in Table 5-1. The Thought Disorder and total problems scales also showed the largest effects of referral status for boys, both accounting for 11% of variance. The Internalizing scale was third, showing a 10% effect.

The effects of referral status on the YSR scales were generally smaller than those found for adolescents on either the CBCL or TRF scales (Achenbach & Edelbrock, 1983, 1986). However, the following scales are likely to be the most helpful in identifying adolescents who resemble our referred versus nonreferred samples, because they showed much larger effects of referral status than of demographic variables: Both sexes—Delinquent, Depressed, Thought Disorder, Unpopular, Internalizing, Externalizing, and total problem score; girls only—Somatic Complaints.

For most purposes, the total problem score would be the best discriminator, because it encompasses all types of problems. The difference between mean total problem score for referred versus nonreferred adolescents was 17 points for boys and 20 points for girls, as shown in Appendix C.

To provide a more detailed picture of relations between total problem scores and referral status, Table 5-2 shows the probability of particular scores being from our referred sample of each sex. This was determined by tabulating the number of adolescents from our referred and nonreferred samples who had each total problem score. The probabilities shown in Table 5-2 represent the percent of YSRs within each range of scores that were from the referred sample, adjusted for the differences in the sizes of the referred and nonreferred samples.

As Table 5-2 indicates, the percent of YSRs from the referred sample generally increased as the scores increased. After the probability of scores being from the referred sample reached .50 (scores of 50-54 for girls, 55-59 for boys), all the succeeding scores had a probability greater than .50 of being from the referred sample. Nearly all the scores greater than 89 came from the referred sample. Table 5-2 can be used to estimate the likelihood that scores of a particular magnitude reflect deviance severe enough to warrant concern.

Table 5-2
Probability of Total Problem Raw Score
Being from Referred Sample

Problem Score	Boys	Girls
0–9	.23	.09
10–14	.36	.31
15–19	.18	.39
20–24	.45	.31
25–29	.35	.35
30–34	.42	.37
35–39	.36	.28
40–44	.45	.36
45–49	.44	.46
50–54	.45	.51
55–59	.70	.53
60–64	.65	.65
65–69	.64	.68
70–74	.80	.79
75–79	.67	.76
80–84	.75	.63
85–89	.82	.75
90–206	1.00	.97

Note. Referred plus nonreferred N = 754 boys, 740 girls.

Cutoff Scores

Beside viewing criterion-related validity in terms of quantitative associations between referral status and scale scores, users may wish to discriminate more categorically between adolescents likely to resemble our referred sample and those likely to resemble our nonreferred sample. We compared the distributions of total problem scores for our samples of referred adolescents whose YSRs were factor analyzed and the nonreferred adolescents on whom the *T* scores were based. For both sexes, scores falling around the 89th percentile for the normative sample were found to minimize the sum of false positives and false negatives in these samples.

The specific score selected as a cutoff for the top of the clinical range was 68 for boys and 70 for girls. The slightly higher cutoff score for girls reflects the girls' tendency to report somewhat more problems on the YSR than boys did (mean total problem scores = 44 for nonreferred girls versus 39 for nonreferred boys).

For users who wish to discriminate between the "normal" and "clinical" range on the broad-band Internalizing and Externalizing scales, the 89th percentile scores also serve as effective discriminators on these scales. The cutoff scores for Internalizing and Externalizing are listed in Table 5-3, along with the cutoffs for total problem scores.

Table 5-3
Cutoff Points for Internalizing, Externalizing, and
Total Problem Raw Scores

	Problem Raw Scores Greater than These are in the "Clinical Range" [a]		
	Intern.	*Extern.*	*Total*
Boys	27	25	68
Girls	34	23	70

[a] > 89th percentile

For comparison between our demographically-matched samples, Table 5-4 displays the percent of referred and nonreferred adolescents who scored above the cutoffs on each problem scale. The cutoffs for the narrow-band problem scales are at approximately the 98th percentile ($T = 70$), as discussed in Chapter 3. The cutoffs for Internalizing, Externalizing, and total problems are at approximately the 89th percentile. Chi square tests showed that significantly ($p < .005$) more referred than nonreferred adolescents scored above the cutoffs on all scales. The percent of nonreferred adolescents scoring above the cutoffs varies from what is implied by the percentiles defining the cutoffs, for two reasons: *(a)* The clustering of subjects at certain scores on some scales caused percentiles to be skipped in the normative samples on which the cutoffs were based, e.g., percentiles jumped from the 96th to the 99th on the distribution of scores for some narrow-band scales; *(b)* the nonreferred samples shown in Table 5-4 were not identical to the original normative samples but were selected for demographic matching to the referred samples.

Table 5-4
Percent of Adolescents in Matched Referred and Nonreferred Samples Who Scored in the "Clinical Range" on Problem Scales[a]

	Boys		Girls	
	Ref.	*Nonref.*	*Ref.*	*Nonref.*
Scales	*N*=366	*N*=388	*N*=349	*N*=391
Aggressive	9	3	10	3
Delinquent	9	3	11	3
Depressed	11	1	16	2
Self-Destructive/ Identity Problems	8	2	Not scored for girls	
Somatic Complaints	11	2	18	5
Thought Disorder	13	2	28	4
Unpopular	13	2	12	3
≥1 narrow-band scale	33	9	42	12
Internalizing	33	11	39	12
Externalizing	28	10	33	12
Int. and/or Ext.	44	17	57	24
Total Problem Score	30	9	40	12

Note. Significantly more referred than nonreferred adolescents scored in the clinical range on all problem scales, $p < .005$ by chi square.
[a]Clinical range: Narrow band problem scales $T > 70$
Internalizing, Externalizing, Total Problem Score >89th %ile

Across both sexes, the 89th percentile cutoff on the total problem score classified 10.5% of the nonreferred adolescents as being in the clinical range and 65.0% of the referred adolescents as being in the normal range. If nonreferred adolescents who scored above the cutoff are viewed as "false positives" (i.e., the cutoff criterion indicates deviance, but they are not deviant according to the criterion of referral for services), and referred adolescents who scored below the cutoff are viewed as "false negatives," the overall misclassification rate is (10.5% +

65.0%)/2 = 37.8% for samples in which 50% are referred and 50% are not referred. Users can project from these figures the misclassification rates expected for other proportions of deviant adolescents. If 90% of the adolescents in a population are not deviant, for example, the overall misclassification rate would be $(90\% \times .105) + (10\% \times .65) = 16\%$.

(The remainder of this chapter can be skipped by readers not interested in the discriminative power of different procedures.)

For the CBCL and TRF, we compared the accuracy of classification achieved by using the total problem scores with the accuracy achieved by using the cutoffs on competence and adaptive functioning (Achenbach & Edelbrock, 1983, 1986). On the CBCL, the total misclassification rate of 17.9% for the problem score alone was considerably better than the misclassification rate of 26.4% for the competence score alone. On the TRF, the total misclassification rate for the problem score and adaptive score were very similar (27.8% versus 27.5%).

The most accurate classifications via the CBCL and TRF were achieved by using the following three categories: *(a)* Individuals who were in the *clinical range on both* the competence (or adaptive) score and the problem score; *(b)* individuals who were in the normal range on one score but the clinical range on the other; *(c)* individuals who were in the *normal range on both* the competence (or adaptive) score and the problem score. By using an intermediate category for individuals whose scores were mixed with respect to the normal and clinical range, the total misclassification rate was reduced to 9% for the CBCL (with 26.8% in the intermediate category) and 18.7% for the TRF (with 17.7% in the intermediate category). By including TRF ratings for academic performance and using an intermediate category for pupils who had one or two of the three scores in the clinical range, the TRF misclassification rate was reduced to 12.9%, with 33.6% in the intermediate category.

Because effective cutoff points could not be established on the YSR competence scales, we could not use a combination of YSR problem and competence cutoffs to categorize adolescents. Instead, we performed discriminant analyses to compare the accuracy of classification achieved with a quantitative combination of competence and problem scores, as described next.

Discriminant Analysis

Discriminant analysis derives weights for predictor variables to maximize their collective correlation with a predefined classification of subjects in a particular sample. By applying the weights derived in one sample to the classification of subjects in a second sample, we can determine the accuracy with which the weighting of the predictors discriminates between criterion groups. It is necessary to test *(cross-validate)* in a second sample the weights that were derived in the derivation sample, because chance variation peculiar to the derivation sample affects the weights and discriminative power it produces. By applying the weights derived in one sample to a second sample, we can correct for decreases in classification accuracy arising from chance differences between samples.

To form separate samples for derivation and cross-validation of the discriminant weights, we randomly divided our referred and nonreferred adolescents into two subsamples of each sex. A discriminant function was then computed for one sample of each sex by using the total problem score and the two most discriminating competence scores—the Social scale and school performance—as the predictors of group membership, i. e., referred versus nonreferred. (All the cross-validated discriminant functions discussed in this chapter were significant at $p < .001$.)

After weights for the three predictors had been derived in one subsample of each sex, they were used to classify the subjects in the other subsample of each sex. To determine the misclassification rates, we compared actual referral status with classification according to the discriminant functions. Averaged across boys and girls, the mean false positive rate was 28.2% and false negative rate was 37.2%, for an overall misclassification rate of 33.0%. This is somewhat better than the total misclassification rate of 37.8% obtained by using the cutoff on the total problem score alone. In improving overall classification accuracy via the discriminant function, the false positives increased from 10.5% to 28.7%, whereas the false negatives dropped from 65.0% to 37.2%, as compared to classification based on the total problem cutoff alone.

Because the YSR competence scores make only a limited

contribution even when weighted via discriminant functions, we also tested the discriminative power of the problem items and socially desirable items listed on pages 3 and 4 of the YSR. Using randomly selected subsamples of the referred and non-referred adolescents, we computed a discriminant function for each sex in which all individual items were included that reduced Wilks's lambda by at least .001. This included 47 problem and socially desirable items for boys and 43 for girls.

The remaining subsamples of each sex were then classified using the weights obtained in the derivation subsamples. Averaged across boys and girls, the mean false positive rate was 19.7%, false negative rate was 25.3%, and total misclassification rate was 22.5%. This represents a considerable improvement over the misclassification rate of 37.8% using the total problem score alone. The cross-validated 22.5% misclassification rate obtained with the discriminant functions for problem items and socially desirable items is similar to the 21.8% obtained with discriminant functions for the TRF and 22.4% obtained with a combination of cutoffs on the TRF academic performance, adaptive functioning, and total problem scores. It is not as good as the 17.9% misclassification rate obtained with the CBCL total problem cutoff alone or the 15.5% obtained when using the CBCL competence and problem cutoffs together. Nevertheless, it indicates that a weighted combination of YSR items can produce good discrimination between referred and non-referred adolescents. The addition of the YSR school score reduced the cross-validated misclassification rate to 20.1%, although the fact that some older adolescents are out of school limits the utility of discriminant functions that include school scores. (Contact Dr. Achenbach for information on computer programs for applying the weights derived in our discriminant functions.)

Beside demonstrating reasonably good discriminative power for combinations of the YSR items, the discriminant analyses also indicated the specific items that were most strongly associated with referral status. For both sexes, the item contributing most was *9. I can't get my mind off certain thoughts (describe).* As detailed in Chapter 6, this was also the item that discriminated best between referred and nonreferred adolescents in analyses of covariance that controlled for differences associated with sex, age, race, and SES. Although comparisons reported in Chapter 6 show that item 9 was a strong discriminator on the CBCL and TRF, as well as on the YSR, it was outweighed by several other items on those instruments. It thus appears to have exceptional importance in self-reports.

Of the five items making the greatest contributions to the discriminant functions, the others were: Both sexes—25. *I don't get along with other kids*; boys only—50. *I am too fearful or anxious; 65. I refuse to talk; 81. I steal at home*; girls only—14. *I cry a lot; 24. I don't eat as well as I should*; and 76. *I sleep less than most kids.*

In summary, cross-validated weights derived from discriminant analyses of individual problem and socially desirable items produced considerably better classification as referred versus nonreferred (22.5% error rate) than did the 89th percentile cutoff on the total problem score (37.8% error rate). The discriminant functions also revealed that YSR item 9. *I can't get my mind off certain thoughts* discriminated more strongly between referred and nonreferred adolescents than any other single item. This finding was borne out by analyses of covariance controlling for demographic variables (reported in Chapter 6).

Although the item weightings obtained in the discriminant functions produced an overall lower error rate than the cutoff scores did for samples that are 50% referred and 50% nonreferred, the errors were distributed differently. Using the cutoff score, 10.5% of nonreferred adolescents resembled the referred sample (false positives), while 65% of referred adolescents resembled the nonreferred sample (false negatives). Using the cross-validated discriminant functions, the mean error rates were 19.7% false positive and 25.3% false negative.

The effects of the false positive and negative rates depend on base rates for deviance in particular populations. In a population where 80% are not deviant (i.e., 80% are true negatives) and 20% are deviant (i.e., 20% true positives), for example, the error rate obtained with the cutoff score would be $(80\% \times .105) + (20\% \times .65) = 21.4\%$. The corresponding error rate for the discriminant function would be $(80\% \times .197) + (20\% \times .243) =$

20.9%. Although both these error rates approximate the 20% misclassification rate obtained if everyone were classified as nondeviant (a "base rate" prediction), most users are likely to consider one type of error less desirable than another. If it is important to maximize identification of individuals needing help even at the expense of a relatively large false positive rate, for example, the discriminant function would be preferable to a base rate procedure in which everyone is classified as nondeviant. This is because the base rate procedure would miss 100% of deviant individuals, whereas the discriminant function would identify 75% of them.

For most screening purposes, a multiple gating procedure would be used in which an inexpensive measure such as the YSR would be administered to large numbers of adolescents at one stage, but other methods would be used as well. It should also be remembered that cutoff and screening procedures impose categorical classifications (e. g., deviant versus nondeviant) on quantitative variation. Cutoff points and discriminant functions can therefore be raised or lowered to alter the proportion of a sample identified as deviant or nondeviant according to the user's aims.

Narrow-Band Problem Scales

As discussed in Chapter 2, we followed the CBCL and TRF practice of setting cutoffs for the YSR narrow-band problem scales at the 98th percentile ($T = 70$) of our normative samples. We set these cutoffs higher than those for Internalizing, Externalizing, and total problem score, because a particular degree of deviance on a single narrow-band scale is less likely to be a reliable basis for concern than the same degree of deviance in the multiple areas represented by the broad-band and total problem scores. Table 5-4 shows the percent of adolescents in our demographically-similar referred and nonreferred samples who scored above the cutoff for each scale.

Because each narrow-band scale represents a relatively specific class of problems, the discriminative power of each scale taken alone is less than that of the total problem score. If a score above the cutoff on one or more of the narrow-band scales is used as a criterion for deviance, however, the mean false positive rate is 10.7%, while the mean false negative rate is 62.7%. This yields an overall misclassification rate of 36.7%, which is close to the 37.8% misclassification rate obtained with the cutoff on the total problem score. The presence of at least one narrow-band scale score above the 98th percentile cutoff should carry about the same weight as a total problem score above the 89th percentile cutoff in alerting the user to a need for help. Nevertheless, deviance on the YSR should never be the sole basis for judgment.

Internalizing and Externalizing

The Internalizing and Externalizing scores comprise broad-band groupings of the YSR's narrow-band scales. Table 5-4 shows that the 89th percentile cutoffs for the Internalizing scale provide approximately the same degree of discrimination between referred and nonreferred adolescents of each sex as the 89th percentile cutoff on the total problem score. If we classify as deviant those adolescents who score above the cutoff on either or both broad band scales, the mean false positive rate is 20.4% and false negative rate is 49.5%. This yields a mean misclassification rate of 35%, compared to 37.8% for the 89th percentile total problem cutoff used alone and 36.7% for having one or more narrow band scale scores above their 98th percentile cutoffs.

SUMMARY

The *content validity* of the YSR items was evaluated in terms of whether they were related to concerns about adolescents' need for mental health services. The YSR competence and problem items are based on CBCL items that were developed from previous research, pilot testing in clinics, and feedback from parents, paraprofessionals, and clinicians. We found significantly ($p < .01$) lower scores on 10 of the 17 competence items and higher scores on 89 of the 102 problem items for referred than nonreferred adolescents. On the competence items regarding number of sports and nonsports activities, however, referred adolescents scored themselves higher than nonreferred adolescents. These two items and the Activities and total competence scales of which they are a part cannot, therefore, be viewed as indices of need for mental health services. Of the remaining items, prospective users should judge whether their content is suitable for their intended purposes.

We concluded that the competence scores may be useful in describing particular strengths and weaknesses acknowledged by individual adolescents, but that they should not be used in determining clinical status.

Using referral for mental health services as a criterion, we presented evidence for *criterion-related validity* in terms of significantly ($p < .01$) higher scores for referred than nonreferred adolescents on all YSR problem scales. Referred adolescents also obtained significantly ($p < .01$) lower scores than nonreferred adolescents on the Social scale and school performance. Demographic effects on all these scales were smaller than the effects associated with referral status. Procedures were presented for discriminating between YSRs that resemble those from our referred versus nonreferred samples. Misclassification rates vary with the proportion of true positives and true negatives in a population, as well as with the cutoff points chosen.

Chapter 6
Item Scores

Beside being scored on scales of the YSR profile, the YSR items provide self-reports of specific problems and competencies that generally parallel those scored by parents on the CBCL. The CBCL items concerning special class placement, grade repetition, and other school problems, plus 16 specific problem items, were not deemed appropriate to ask adolescents. Other CBCL items were modified to make them more appropriate for adolescents to report about themselves, as shown in Figures 1-1 and 1-2. Even items that are worded similarly on the CBCL and YSR, however, may reflect different phenomena when reported by parents about their adolescents than when reported by adolescents about themselves. This is because parents and adolescents may be aware of different aspects of the adolescents' behavior and feelings. Furthermore, adolescents and their parents may differ in their thresholds for reporting particular aspects of functioning. Each may be more willing or able to report certain types of problems than the other is.

To determine which YSR items discriminate between adolescents referred for mental health services and demographically similar nonreferred adolescents, we performed analyses like those previously reported for CBCL and TRF items (Achenbach & Edelbrock, 1981, 1986). For every item, we performed an analysis of covariance (ANCOVA) on the raw scores for adolescents grouped by age, sex, and referral status. We partialled out the effects of race (black versus white) and SES (Hollingshead, 1975, parental occupation scores ranging from 1 to 9) by including them as covariates. Ages were grouped by years 11-12, 13-14, 15-16, and 17-18, using the same 715 referred and 779 nonreferred adolescents as described in Chapter 5, for a total N = 1494. The ANCOVA design was thus 4 (age) $\times$ 2 (sex) $\times$ 2 (referral status), with race (black versus white) and SES (9-step scale) as covariates.

Because ages 11-18 were grouped in 2-year intervals, there were 100 YSRs per cell, except at ages 11-12 for referred girls, where $N = 96$, and ages 17-18, where $N = 53$ for referred girls,

66 for referred boys, 88 for nonreferred boys, and 91 for non-referred girls. The smaller Ns for 17- and 18-year-olds were due to the difficulty of making contact with youth in this age range, both through child/adolescent mental health services and through home visits.

Table 6-1 presents the results for each competence item and the Activities, Social, and total competence scores. Table 6-2 presents the results for each specific problem item, the 16 socially desirable items, and the total problem scores. The findings are presented graphically in Figures 6-1 and 6-2. The large sample provided high statistical power, the number of analyses was large, and we found numerous significant effects. We have therefore designated as significant only those effects that reached the $p < .01$ level. Furthermore, because some effects can reach even the $p < .01$ level by chance, we have marked with a superscript g the number of $p < .01$ effects expected by chance for the number of analyses conducted, using a .01 protection level (Sakoda, Cohen, & Beall, 1954). In each column of Table 6-1, superscript g marks the 2 effects that were most likely to have reached the .01 level by chance in 20 analyses, because they had the smallest F values. In each column of Table 6-2, super-script g marks the 5 effects out of 119 that were most likely to be chance.

Table 6-1
Percent of Variance Accounted for by Significant ($p < .01$)
Effects of Referral Status and Demographic Variables in
ANCOVAs of Competence Items

Item	Main Effects[a]			Covariate[e]
	Ref. Stat.[b]	Sex[c]	Age[d]	SES[f]
I.A. Number of sports	$<1^{gR}$	2^M	2^Y	—
B. Participation in sports	—	4^M	1^Y	—
C. Skill in sports	—	1^M	1^Y	—
II.A. Number of nonsports activities	3^R	—	2^Y	$<1^g$
B. Participation in activities	—	—	—	—
C. Skill in activities	—	—	—	—

Table 6-1 (Cont'd)

Item	Ref. Stat.[b]	Sex[c]	Age[d]	SES[f]
		Main Effects[a]		Covariate[e]
III.A. Number of organizations	1^N	—	$<1^{gY}$	4
B. Participation in organizations	1^N	—	$<1^Y$	—
IV.A. Number of jobs	—	—	1^Y	3
B. Job performance	1^N	$<^{gF}$	—	—
V.1. Number of friends	2^N	—	—	—
2. Contacts with friends	3^N	$<1^M$	—	—
VI.a. Get along with siblings	—	—	1^O	—
b. Get along with other kids	3^N	—	—	—
c. Get along with parents	6^N	—	1^Y	
d. Do things by self	—	—	—	—
VII. School performance	7^N	—	—	1
Activities Scale	1^R	—	2^Y	1
Social Scale	5^N	$<1^{gM}$	$<1^{gY}$	$<1^g$
Total Competence	$<1^{gN}$	—	1^Y	1

Note. Items are designated with summary labels for their content; numbers in table indicate percent of variance in scores accounted for by each independent variable and covariate where the effect was significant at $p<.01$.
[a] Interactions are not listed, because only 1 out of 60 was significant, which is less than expected by chance.
[b] N = higher scores for nonreferred youth; R = higher scores for referred youth.
[c] F = higher scores for females; M = higher scores for males.
[d] O = higher scores for older youth; Y = higher scores for younger youth;
[e] Race as a covariate had no significant effects on any competence scores.
[f] All significant SES effects reflect higher scores for upper SES.
[g] Not significant when corrected for number of analyses.

To indicate the magnitude of the significant effects, Tables 6-1 and 6-2 list the percent of variance accounted for by each effect. According to Cohen's (1977) standards, ANCOVA effects accounting for 1-5.9% of variance are small, 5.9-13.8% are medium, and $\geq13.8\%$ are large. (Note that the percent of variance accounted for by ANCOVA effects is not directly comparable to the variance accounted for by the partial correlations shown in Table 5-1; the magnitude of effects is determined in different ways by different combinations of variables in the partial correlations and ANCOVAs.)

Table 6-2
Percent of Variance Accounted for by Significant ($p<.01$) Effects of Referral Status and Demographic Variables in ANCOVAs of Problems and Socially Desirable Items

Item	Main Effects Ref. Stat.[b]	Sex[c]	Age[d]	Interactions[a] RA	RS	SA	Covariates Race[e]	SES[f]
1. Acts too young	1	—	1^Y	—	—	—	—	—
2. Allergy	—	—	—	—	—	—	—	—
3. Argues a lot	1	—	1^Y	—	—	—	—	—
4. Asthma	—	—	—	—	—	—	—	—
5. Act like opposite sex	—	2^F	—	—	—	—	—	—
6. Likes animals (soc. des.)	—	—	1^Y	—	—	—	$<1^W$	—
7. Brags	$<1^g$	$<1^M$	—	—	—	—	—	—
8. Can't concentrate	5	—	—	—	—	—	—	—
9. Can't get mind off thoughts	20	—	—	—	1	—	—	—
10. Trouble sitting still	1	—	—	—	—	—	$<1^W$	—
11. Too dependent	<1	—	1^{NL}	—	—	—	—	—
12. Lonely	6	3^F	$<1^{gO}$	—	—	—	—	—
13. Confused	7	2^F	—	—	—	<1	—	—
14. Cries	6	11^F	—	—	$<1^g$	1	$<1^W$	—

Note. Items are designated with summary labels for their content; numbers in table indicate percent of variance in scores accounted for by each independent variable and covariate where the effect was significant at $p<.01$. Soc. des. indicates socially desirable items excluded from the problem scores.

[a]RA = referral status x age; RS = referral status x sex; SA = sex x age; see Fig. 6-2 for shapes of interactions.

[b]All significant effects reflect higher scores by referred youth on problem items and lower scores on socially desirable items.

[c]F = higher scores for females; M = higher scores for males.

[d]O = higher scores for older youth; Y = higher scores for younger youth; NL = nonlinear effect of age.

[e]B = higher scores for blacks; W = higher scores for whites.

[f]L = higher scores for lower SES; U = higher scores for upper SES.

[g]Not significant when corrected for number of analyses.

Table 6-2 (Cont'd)

Item	Ref. Stat.[b]	Sex[c]	Age[d]	RA	RS	SA	Race[e]	SES[f]
		Main Effects		Interactions[a]			Covariates	
15. Honest (soc. des.)	—	—	2^O	—	—	—	—	—
16. Mean to others	3	—	—	—	—	—	—	—
17. Daydreams	1	$<1^F$	2^O	—	—	—	—	—
18. Harms self	5	3^F	—	—	$<1^g$	$<1^g$	—	—
19. Tries to get attention	1	—	—	$<1^g$	—	—	—	—
20. Destroys own things	3	$<1^{gM}$	—	—	—	—	—	—
21. Destroys others' things	2	$<1^{gM}$	—	—	—	—	—	$<1^L$
22. Disobeys parents	3	—	—	—	—	—	—	—
23. Disobeys at school	4	1^M	—	—	—	—	—	$<1^L$
24. Doesn't eat well	—	2^F	1^O	—	—	$<1^g$	—	—
25. Doesn't get along	8	—	—	—	—	—	—	—
26. Lacks guilt	$<1^g$	—	—	—	—	—	—	—
27. Jealous	—	1^F	$<1^O$	—	—	—	1^W	$<1^{gU}$
28. Willing to help (soc. des.)	—	1^F	—	—	—	—	—	—
29. Fears	—	$<1^F$	$<1^{gNL}$	—	—	—	—	—
30. Fears school	<1	$<1^F$	—	—	—	—	$<1^{gW}$	—
31. Fears impulses	2	—	$<1^{gY}$	—	—	—	$<1^{gW}$	—
32. Needs to be perfect	<1	1^F	—	—	—	—	—	$<1^U$
33. Feels unloved	5	2^F	—	—	$<1^g$	—	—	—
34. Feels persecuted	4	$<1^F$	—	—	—	—	—	—
35. Feels worthless	5	2^F	—	—	—	—	—	—
36. Accident-prone	<1	$<1^M$	2^Y	—	—	—	—	—
37. Fighting	2	$<1^M$	2^Y	—	—	1	—	1^L
38. Is teased	4	—	4^Y	2	—	—	$<1^W$	$<1^{gL}$
39. Hangs around kids who get in trouble	2	1^M	—	—	—	—	—	2^L
40. Hears things	5	—	—	—	—	—	—	$<1^L$
41. Acts without thinking	2	—	—	—	—	$<1^g$	—	—
42. Likes to be alone	2	1^F	$<1^{gO}$	—	—	—	—	—
43. Lying or cheating	2	—	—	—	—	—	—	—

See page 64 for footnotes to Table .

Table 6-2 (Cont'd)

Item	Ref. Stat.[b]	Sex[c]	Age[d]	RA	RS	SA	Race[e]	SES[f]
		Main Effects		*Interactions*[a]			*Covariates*	
44. Bites fingernails	1	—	1^Y	—	—	—	—	$<1^L$
45. Nervous	4	2^F	—	—	—	—	$<1^W$	—
46. Nervous movements	3	—	—	—	—	—	—	—
47. Nightmares	1	1^F	1^Y	—	—	<1	—	—
48. Not liked	5	—	1^Y	—	—	—	—	—
49. Can do things better (soc. des.)	—	1^M	—	—	—	—	$<1^B$	—
50. Fearful or anxious	4	—	—	—	—	—	$<1^{gW}$	—
51. Dizzy	3	$<1^{gF}$	—	—	—	—	—	—
52. Feels too guilty	3	$<1^F$	—	—	—	—	—	—
53. Eats too much	—	2^F	1^Y	—	—	—	—	—
54. Overtired	2	$<1^F$	1^O	—	—	—	$<1^W$	—
55. Overweight	1	6^F	—	—	$<1^g$	1	—	—
56a. Aches or pains	2	—	—	—	—	1	—	—
56b. Headaches	3	3^F	1^Y	—	—	1	—	$<1^L$
56c. Nausea, feels sick	4	$<1^F$	$<1^Y$	—	—	—	—	—
56d. Eye problems	3	—	—	—	—	—	$<1^{gB}$	—
56e. Skin problems	—	$<1^{gF}$	—	—	—	—	—	—
56f. Stomachaches	3	3^F	—	$<1^g$	—	1	—	—
56g. Vomiting	1	—	1^Y	1	—	—	—	$<1^L$
57. Attacks people	2	—	—	—	—	—	—	$<1^L$
58. Picking	<1	—	1^Y	—	—	—	—	—
59. Friendly (soc. des.)	—	$<1^F$	—	—	—	—	—	—
60. Likes new things (soc. des.)	—	—	—	—	—	—	—	—
61. Poor school work	5	—	—	—	—	—	—	$<1^L$
62. Clumsy	1	—	—	—	—	—	—	—
63. Prefers older kids	3	$<1^F$	3°	—	—	—	—	—
64. Prefers younger kids	1	—	1^{NL}	—	—	—	—	—
65. Refuses to talk	5	—	—	—	—	—	—	$<1^L$
66. Repeats actions	6	—	—	—	—	—	—	—
67. Runs away from home	7	1^F	$<1^{NL}$	—	—	—	—	—
68. Screams a lot	3	4^F	—	$<1^g$	—	—	—	—

See page 64 for footnotes to Table .

Table 6-2 (Cont'd)

Item	Ref. Stat.[b]	Sex[c]	Age[d]	RA	RS	SA	Race[e]	SES[f]
		Main Effects			Interactions[a]		Covariates	
69. Secretive	4	1^F	$<1^O$	—	—	$<1^g$	—	—
70. Sees things	3	—	—	—	—	—	—	$<1^L$
71. Self-conscious	$<1^g$	4^F	—	—	—	—	$<1^W$	—
72. Sets fires	<1	2^M	—	—	—	—	—	—
73. Works well with hands (soc. des.)	—	3^M	—	—	—	—	—	—
74. Shows off	$<1^g$	2^M	—	—	—	—	—	—
75. Shy	—	1^F	—	—	—	—	—	—
76. Sleeps little	1	—	—	—	—	—	—	—
77. Sleeps much	1	—	—	—	—	—	—	$<1^L$
78. Good imagination (soc. des.)	—	—	—	—	—	—	—	—
79. Speech problem	2	—	—	—	—	—	—	$<1^L$
80. Stands up for rights (soc. des.)	—	—	—	—	—	—	—	—
81. Steals at home	3	—	—	—	—	—	—	—
82. Steals outside home	2	$<1^M$	—	—	—	—	—	$<1^L$
83. Stores up unneeded things	2	—	—	—	—	—	—	$<1^{gL}$
84. Strange behavior	7	—	—	—	—	—	—	—
85. Strange thoughts	4	—	—	—	—	—	—	—
86. Stubborn	1	3^F	4°	—	—	$<1^g$	—	—
87. Moody	3	3^F	2^O	—	—	<1	—	—
88. Enjoys others (soc. des.)	1	$<1^F$	—	—	—	—	—	—
89. Suspicious	<1	—	—	—	—	—	—	—
90. Swearing	2	$<1^M$	6°	—	—	—	$<1^W$	—
91. Suicidal thoughts	4	2^F	—	—	$<1^g$	<1	—	—
92. Likes to make others laugh (soc. des.)	—	$<1^F$	—	—	—	—	—	—
93. Talks too much	—	5^F	—	<1	—	—	$<1^W$	—
94. Teases a lot	—	$<1^{gM}$	—	—	—	—	—	—

See page 64 for footnotes to Table .

Table 6-2 (Cont'd)

Item	Ref. Stat.[b]	Sex[c]	Age[d]	RA	RS	SA	Race[e]	SES[f]
		Main Effects			*Interactions*[a]		*Covariates*	
95. Hot temper	3	—	$<1^{gNL}$	—	—	<1	—	$<1^{L}$
96. Thinks about sex	<1	3^{M}	4°	—	—	—	—	—
97. Threatens people	4	1^{M}	—	—	—	—	—	$<1^{gL}$
98. Likes to help (soc. des.)	—	3^{F}	—	—	—	—	—	—
99. Concerned w. neat & clean	—	2^{F}	—	$<1^{g}$	—	—	$<1^{B}$	$<1^{L}$
100. Trouble sleeping	3	1^{F}	—	—	—	—	—	—
101. Truancy	3	—	5°	—	—	—	—	$<1^{gL}$
102. Lacks energy	1	1^{F}	—	—	—	—	—	—
103. Unhappy, sad, depressed	8	4^{F}	$<1^{O}$	—	—	—	—	—
104. Loud	1	—	$<1^{Y}$	—	—	—	—	—
105. Alcohol, drugs	2	—	10°	—	—	—	—	—
106. Fair to others (soc. des.)	—	1^{F}	—	—	—	—	—	—
107. Enjoys jokes (soc. des.)	2		—	—	—	—	—	—
108. Takes life easy (soc. des.)	—	—	—	—	—	—	—	—
109. Tries to help (soc. des.)	$<1^{g}$	3^{F}	—	—	—	—	—	—
110. Wishes to be opposite sex	—	3^{F}	—	—	—	—	—	—
111. Keeps from getting involved	2	—	—	—	—	—	$<1^{B}$	—
112. Worries a lot	4	5^{F}	—	$<1^{g}$	—	<1	$<1^{gW}$	—
Total Problem Score	12	2^{F}	—	—	—	<1	—	$<1^{L}$

See page 64 for footnotes to Table .

EFFECTS OF DEMOGRAPHIC VARIABLES

The ANCOVAs were designed to separate the effects of age, sex, race, and SES from differences in YSR responses by referred and nonreferred adolescents. We shall first consider the effects of the demographic variables before turning to the differences between responses by referred versus nonreferred adolescents.

Competence Scores

For the competence scores, the 60 analyses of 2-way interactions and 20 analyses of 3-way interactions between referral status, age, and sex yielded only one significant effect. This effect accounted for <1% of the variance between referral status and sex for number of sports. Because one significant effect was less than expected by chance and there were no significant effects of race in the ANCOVAs of competence scores, Table 6-1 does not list any effects for interactions or race.

As Table 6-1 shows, SES effects were significant for 7 of the 20 competence items. All of these reflected higher scores for upper SES than lower SES adolescents, a finding that is consistent with the higher scores obtained by upper SES adolescents in reports by parents and teachers (Achenbach & Edelbrock, 1981, 1986).

There were significant age differences for 12 of the 20 competence scores listed in Table 6-1. All of these reflected slightly higher scores for younger adolescents than older adolescents, except for ratings on getting along with siblings. The findings indicate somewhat greater involvement in sports, other recreational activities, organizations, and jobs and chores among younger than older adolescents.

Significant sex differences occurred on 6 of the 20 competence scores, with boys reporting more sports, more and better participation in sports, more contacts with friends, and higher total Social scores. Girls, on the other hand, rated themselves as performing better than boys in jobs and chores. None of the demographic effects accounted for more than 4% of the variance in competence scores.

Problem Scores

Unlike the competence scores, the problem items did show some significant effects of race, as well as some significant interactions between referral status, sex, and age, as listed in Table 6-2. (Because only one 3-way interaction was significant in 119 ANCOVAs, we regard it as a chance finding.) The largest effects of race and 2-way interactions accounted for only 2% of variance, while most accounted for <1% of variance. Of the 16 problem items showing significant effects of race, whites scored themselves higher (indicating more problems) on 13. These differences were too small, however, to create a significant effect of race on total problem score or more than chance racial differences on any scale score, as shown by the analyses of scale scores listed separately for each sex in Table 5-1 of Chapter 5.

Of the 23 problem items showing significant SES effects, lower SES adolescents scored themselves higher on 21. This is consistent with CBCL and TRF findings, where parents and teachers also reported slightly more problems for lower SES than upper SES children and adolescents (Achenbach & Edelbrock, 1981, 1986; Achenbach, Verhulst, Baron, & Akkerhuis, 1987; Achenbach, Verhulst, Edelbrock, Baron, & Akkerhuis, 1987). The SES effect on YSR total problem score was of the same very small magnitude (<1% of variance) as found on the CBCL total problem score.

As Table 6-2 shows, the main effects of age and sex were larger and more numerous than the effects of race, SES, or interactions between variables. Although many of the age and sex effects were very small, the following items met Cohen's (1977) criteria for medium effects, with the effect size shown in parentheses: Age—*90. I swear or use dirty language* (6%); *105. I use alcohol or drugs* (10%); sex—*14. I cry a lot* (11%); *55. I am overweight* (6%). Both of the age effects reflected higher scores for older adolescents, while both of the sex effects reflected higher scores for girls.

Across all problem items, 15 age effects involved higher scores for younger adolescents, 15 involved higher scores for older adolescents, and 5 were nonlinear effects. There was no significant age effect on total problem score. Of the significant sex effects on problem items, 42 involved higher scores for girls, while 14 involved higher scores for boys. Girls also obtained significantly higher total problem scores, with this sex effect accounting for 2% of variance.

In summary, differences between self-reports by black and white adolescents were small enough to be negligible. SES differences reflected a consistent but small tendency for lower SES adolescents to report fewer competencies and more problems than upper SES adolescents, as also found in parent and teacher ratings. Most age effects on competence items reflected a small tendency for younger adolescents to obtain higher scores than older adolescents. Age effects on the problem items were equally divided as to direction and were small, except for medium effects reflecting higher scores for older adolescents on swearing and use of alcohol and drugs, not surprisingly. The most numerous demographic differences involved higher scores for girls on 42 problem items and the total problem score, whereas boys had higher scores on 14 problem items. The greater differences associated with sex than with any of the other demographic variables supports our decision to derive problem scales and norms separately for boys and girls.

EFFECTS OF REFERRAL STATUS

Because the ANCOVAs were designed to separate demographic effects from referral status, we will now consider the relations between referral status and item scores independently of the demographics. (Note that Table 5-1 in Chapter 5 presents analyses of demographic variables and referral status for all scale scores separately for each sex, reflecting the separate standardization of scales for boys and girls.)

Competence Scores

Table 6-1 shows significant differences between referred and nonreferred adolescents on 13 of the 20 competence scores. Ten of the significant differences reflected higher scores for non-referred adolescents, with the largest effects being for how well

they get along with parents (6% of variance), school performance (7% of variance), and the Social scale score (5% of
variance). Three of the significant differences reflected higher
scores for referred adolescents on number of sports (<1% of
variance), number of nonsports activities (3% of variance), and
the Activities scale score (1% of variance).

The difference for number of sports would be excluded when
correcting for the number of significant effects expected by
chance, and the other two differences reflecting higher scores
for referred adolescents were small effects. However, the tendency for referred adolescents to report more activities is consistent with Zimet and Farley's (1987) finding of more favorable
self-ratings for activities by disturbed than normal children on
Harter's (1982) Perceived Competence Scale for Children. These
findings bear out our conclusion in Chapter 5 that the YSR
Activities scale does not discriminate effectively between referred
and nonreferred adolescents. As shown in Table 5-1 for the
analyses of each sex separately, the tendency for referred adolescents to score higher on the Activities scale was significant only
for girls. Yet, because there was no significant difference between
referred and nonreferred boys on the Activities scale, this scale
cannot serve as an effective discriminator for boys either. The
inclusion of the Activities scale score in the total competence
score also limits the utility of this score for discriminating
between groups.

Our analyses of parents' ratings showed that the number of
sports and amount of participation in nonsports activities discriminated less well than other CBCL competence items between
referred and nonreferred samples (Achenbach & Edelbrock,
1981). The referred samples did receive significantly lower CBCL
scores on these items, however. The CBCL Activities scale
scores were also significantly lower for referred than nonreferred
samples, with referral status accounting for 11% of the variance.
Although this meets Cohen's criteria for a medium effect size, it
was smaller than the very large effects found for the CBCL
Social scale (28%), School scale (30%), and total competence
score (35%). Nevertheless, the CBCL findings indicate that
parents' ratings for activities are more effective discriminators

between referred and nonreferred groups than are adolescents' self-ratings for these same items.

Other studies have shown a general tendency for disturbed children to rate themselves more favorably than parents, teachers, or therapists do on a variety of measures (Kazdin, French, & Unis, 1983; Piers, 1972; Zimet & Farley, 1986). Although the YSR school performance item and most of the social items did show significant differences in favor of non-referred adolescents, the main value of self-ratings of favorable items is probably to indicate what views adolescents are willing to share about their competencies, rather than to assess the competencies themselves. Nevertheless, extremely low competence scores are likely to indicate a need for help in these areas, even if higher scores cannot be taken as evidence against such needs.

Problem Scores

As Table 6-2 shows, all significant differences on problem items reflected higher scores for referred than nonreferred adolescents. The largest effect was on item *9. I can't get my mind off certain thoughts (describe)*, where referral status accounted for 20.3% of the variance, which is a large effect by Cohen's standards. On the CBCL and TRF, this item included the word "obsessions," which was omitted from the YSR because it was apt to be unfamiliar to adolescents. Furthermore, the scoring instructions for the YSR (Appendix A) state that scoring is not restricted to obsessions and that almost anything listed by the adolescent should be scored the way he or she scored it, unless it is more specifically covered by another item. If the respondent wrote "sex" for item *9*, for example, it should be rescored on item *96. I think about sex too much.* By contrast, the scoring instructions for the CBCL and TRF state that item *9* should not be scored for "anything that is clearly not obsessional." (The inclusion of the word "obsessions" and the narrower criteria for CBCL and TRF item *9*, do not require, however, that CBCL and TRF responses must indicate obsessions of clinical degree to warrant being scored.)

As on the YSR, item *9* on the CBCL showed a large effect of referral status, accounting for 15% of the variance. On the TRF, item *9* showed a medium effect of referral status, accounting for 9% of the variance. According to all three types of informants, this item was thus strongly associated with referral status. As depicted in the graph of this item in Figure 6-2, 65.1% of referred adolescents endorsed this item, compared to 18.7% of nonreferred adolescents. For comparison with parent ratings for ages 12-16, the CBCL rates were 55.9% for referred adolescents and 15.9% for nonreferred, just slightly lower than the YSR rates of 57.3% and 18.3% over these ages. As might be expected, TRF rates were lower, being 33.7% for referred adolescents and 9.5% for nonreferred over these ages.

On the YSR, item *103. Unhappy, sad, or depressed* showed the second largest effect, with referral status accounting for 8.4% of the variance. This was the item that showed the greatest discrimination between referred and nonreferred groups in CBCL and TRF ratings, where referral status accounted for 29% and 18% of variance, respectively. Although these were larger effects than found for this item on the YSR, the fact that it showed the second largest effect of all the YSR items indicates that it is important in self-reports, as well as in reports by parents and teachers. Across all ages and both sexes, this item was endorsed by 57.4% of referred adolescents, compared to 32.5% of nonreferred. For ages 12-16, the CBCL rates were 68.6% for referred adolescents and 10.0% for nonreferred. The TRF rates were 58.7% for referred adolescents and 15% for nonreferred. As is evident in Figure 6-2, item *103* was endorsed considerably more often by girls, both referred (68.3%) and nonreferred (41%), than by boys, either referred (46.5%) or nonreferred (24%). The sex difference was significant, accounting for 4% of the variance in item scores. Although parents also reported item *103* for more referred girls than boys (77% versus 60% at ages 12-16), the overall sex difference accounted for <1% of variance in CBCL ratings of this item. There was no significant sex difference in TRF ratings of item *103*.

Item *25. I don't get along with other kids* showed the third largest effect on the YSR, with referral status accounting for 7.8% of the variance. This item was also strongly associated with referral status in parent and teacher ratings, accounting for 22% of variance on the CBCL and 18% on the TRF. Other YSR items showing medium effects of referral status accounting for 6 to 7% of variance included: *12. I feel lonely; 13. I feel confused or in a fog; 14. I cry a lot; 66. I repeat certain actions over and over (describe); 67. I run away from home;* and *84. I do things other people think are strange.* These items all showed medium effects on the CBCL and TRF, too, except items *13* and *14*, which showed large effects on the CBCL.

The YSR total problem score showed an effect of referral status accounting for 12% of variance, which was larger than the effect found for any single item except *9. I can't get my mind off certain thoughts.* Although it reflects a substantial difference between self-reports by referred and nonreferred adolescents, the effect for the YSR total problem score is smaller than the 44% effect found for the CBCL total problem score and the 29% effect for the TRF total problem score.

The main reason for the smaller effect of referral status on YSR scores was the higher problem scores obtained by the nonreferred sample on the YSR than on the CBCL or TRF. The mean total problem scores obtained on the three instruments by nonreferred samples of comparable ages (11 to 16 years) were: YSR = 41.8; CBCL = 17.1; TRF = 19.4. Although the items differ somewhat on the three instruments, there are 17 fewer problem items on the YSR, limiting its maximum problem score to 206, as compared to 240 on the CBCL and TRF. Unlike the high YSR scores by nonreferred adolescents, referred adolescents obtained total problem scores on the YSR much closer to those of the CBCL and TRF, as follows: YSR = 59.5; CBCL = 54.5; TRF = 55.4.

The graph of the total problem score in Figure 6-2 shows more complex patterns for the YSR than found for CBCL and TRF total problem scores, where the patterns were generally similar for referred and nonreferred adolescents of both sexes at each age (Achenbach & Edelbrock, 1981, 1986). At ages 11-12, referred girls and boys obtained very similar total problem scores on the YSR, as did nonreferred girls and boys. At the older ages, however, referred and nonreferred girls obtained higher scores on the YSR than their male counterparts. Although there were substantial differences between referred and nonreferred adolescents of the same sex, nonreferred girls scored almost as high as referred boys at ages 15-16 (mean score = 48.7 for nonreferred girls versus 52.0 for referred boys). It is therefore important to judge an adolescent's total problem score in relation to YSR norms for that adolescent's sex.

Although 89 of the 102 YSR problem items in Table 6-2 showed significant differences between referred and nonreferred adolescents, 13 did not. Five of these—items *2, 4, 5, 99,* and *110*—also failed to show significant differences on the CBCL or were among the five smallest effect sizes that would be excluded when correcting for the number of significant effects expected by chance on the CBCL.

Of the remaining 8 items that did not show significant effects of referral status on the YSR, all but one showed small effects of referral status on the CBCL. The only one that showed a medium effect of referral status (10%) on the CBCL was *27. Easily jealous (I am jealous of others* on the YSR). It was also the only problem item not showing a significant effect on the YSR but showing a medium effect on the TRF, where referral status accounted for 7% of the variance. The one showing the second largest effect on both the CBCL and TRF was *94. Teases a lot (I tease others a lot* on the YSR). Referral status accounted for 5% of the variance in this item on the CBCL and 6% on the TRF. It thus appears that parent and teacher reports of teasing and jealousy offer good discrimination between referred and nonreferred groups, but that self-reports of these problems do not. However, the other 11 problem items that were not significantly associated with referral status on the YSR also showed little or no effect of referral status in parent and teacher ratings.

In summary, referred adolescents scored themselves significantly higher than nonreferred adolescents on most YSR problem items. The largest effects were on item *9. I can't get my mind off certain thoughts* (20%), the total problem score (12%), and item *103. Unhappy, sad, or depressed* (8%), which was the item showing the largest effect of referral status in parent and teacher ratings. Although the differences between referred and nonreferred adolescents were highly significant, referral status generally showed smaller effects than in parent and teacher ratings. This largely reflected the tendency of nonreferred adolescents to report considerably more problems on the YSR than parents did on the CBCL or teachers on the TRF. Referred adolescents, however, did not report many more problems than parents or teachers did. The patterns of reports by adolescents, parents, and teachers can be compared for each item by looking at the graphs shown in Figures 6-1 and 6-2 and the similar graphs shown in our Monograph on the CBCL and our Manual for the TRF (Achenbach & Edelbrock, 1981, 1986).

Socially Desirable Items

The 16 socially desirable items were included on the YSR to replace items inappropriate for adolescents with favorable statements that most adolescents were expected to endorse. These items are not scored on any YSR scales, but are included in Table 6-2 and Figure 6-2 for informational purposes. The graphs in Figure 6-2 show that most referred and nonreferred adolescents did, in fact, endorse the socially desirable items. The only significant effects of referral status were lower self-ratings by referred than nonreferred adolescents on item *88. I enjoy being with other people* (1% of variance), *107. I enjoy a good joke* (2% of variance), and *109. I try to help others when I can* (<1% of variance, which would be excluded when correcting for chance). The differences in the percent of referred and nonreferred adolescents endorsing these three items ranged from 0.8% to 1.5%. As Table 6-2 indicates, small sex differences were evident on nine socially desirable items, while small age and race differences were evident on two. There were no significant SES differences on the socially desirable items, however.

GRAPHIC PORTRAYAL OF FINDINGS

To illustrate the findings graphically, Figure 6-1 depicts mean scores for each competence item and the competence scales according to sex, age, and referral status. Figure 6-2 similarly depicts the mean total problem scores, plus the percent of adolescents who reported each problem and socially desirable item. For clarity of presentation and comparison with our similar displays of CBCL and TRF problem items (Achenbach & Edelbrock, 1981, 1986), Figure 6-2 combines scores of 1 and 2 to show the percent of adolescents who endorsed each item. Appendix E parallels the graphic display, except that it separates the percent of each group who obtained scores of 1 and 2, as well as the sum of these percents for each item.

The data displayed in Figures 6-1 and 6-2 and Appendix E have been standardized to a distribution that is 20% black and 80% white at each data point. Furthermore, to minimize any SES effects, the white group was divided into three SES levels (Hollingshead, 1975, parental occupation scores 1-3.5 versus 4-6.5 versus 7-9). Mean scores were computed within each SES level. We then weighted by 4 the mean for whites at each of the three SES levels and weighted by 3 the overall mean for blacks (small Ns for blacks in some cells precluded separate weighting of each SES level for blacks). Because the total weights sum to 15 (4×3 SES levels for whites, plus $3 \times$ the overall mean score for blacks), we divided the result by 15 to specify each data point shown in Figures 1 and 2 and Appendix E. Except for the lack of SES stratification for blacks, these are the same standardized distributions as used for our graphs of CBCL and TRF items (Achenbach & Edelbrock, 1981, 1986). Standardization of the distributions in this way minimizes any effects of variations in the demographic composition of samples from one data point to another.

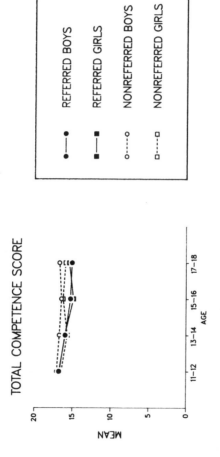

Fig. 6–1. Mean scores for competence items and scales.

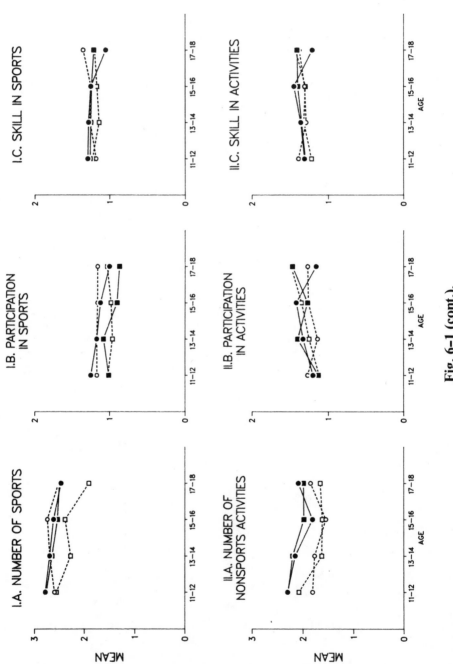

Fig. 6-1 (cont.).

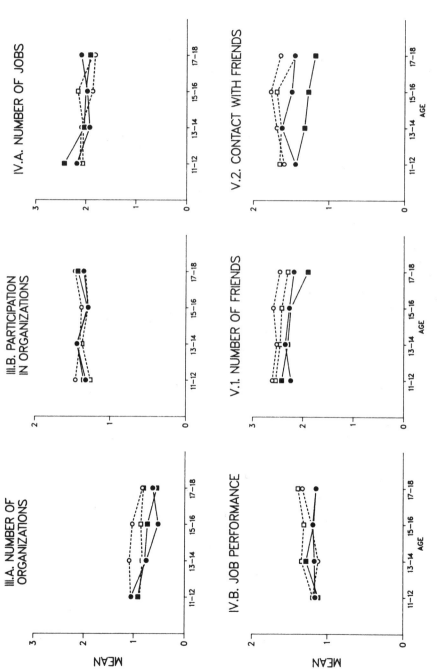

Fig. 6-1 (cont.).

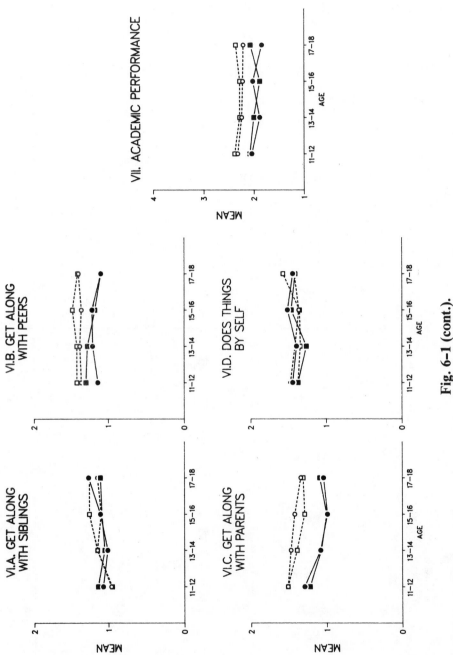

Fig. 6-1 (cont.).

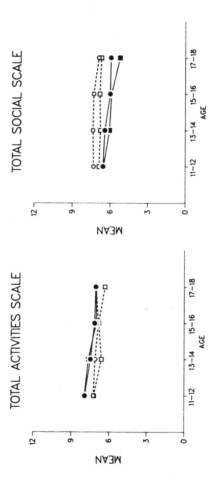

Fig. 6-1 (cont.).

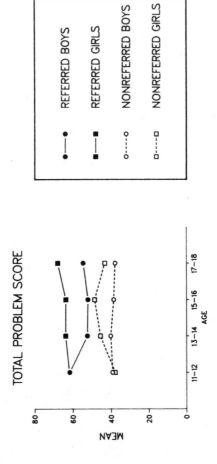

Fig. 6-2. Mean total problem scores and percent of respondents reporting each item. See Appendix E for exact percent scoring themselves *1* and *2* on each item. *Socially desirable items.

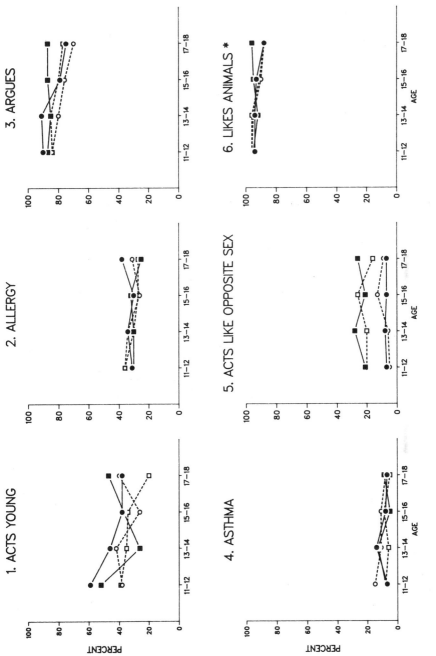

Fig. 6-2 (cont.).

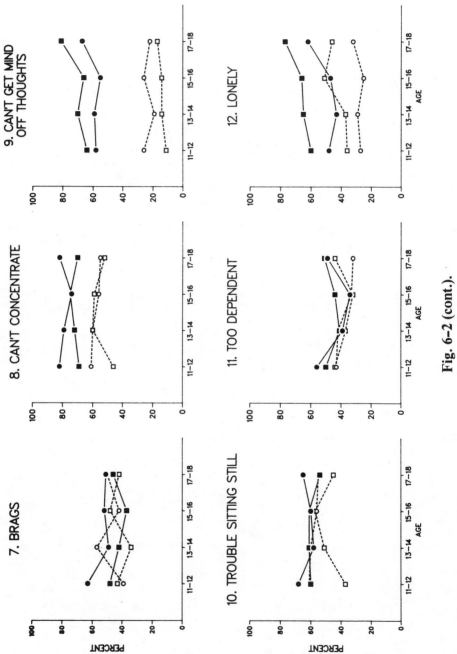

Fig. 6-2 (cont.).

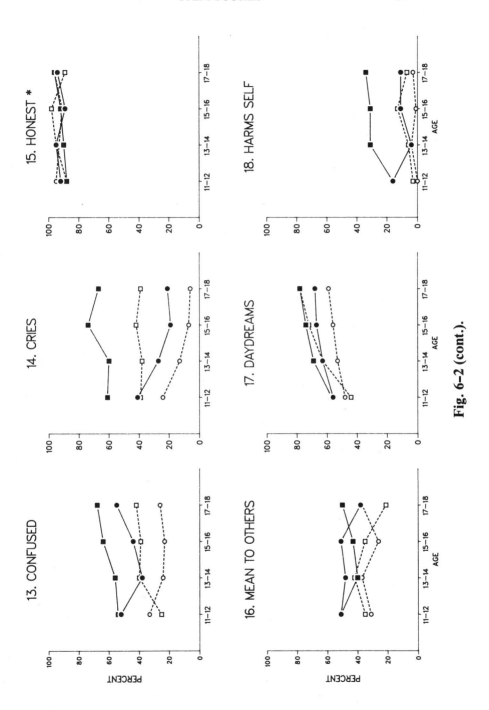

Fig. 6-2 (cont.).

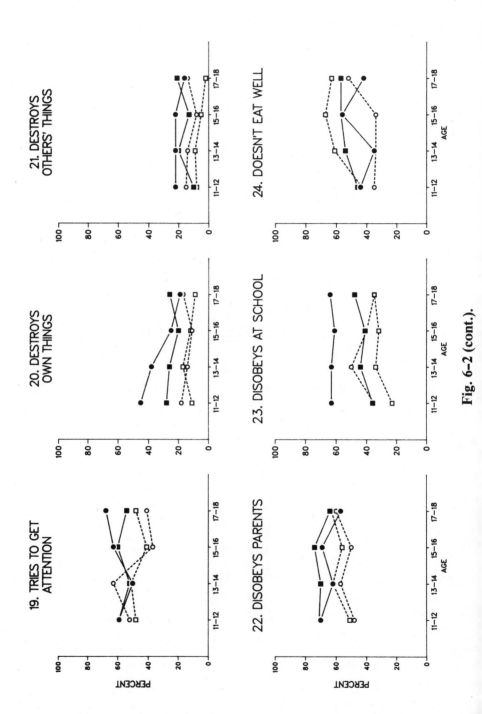

Fig. 6-2 (cont.).

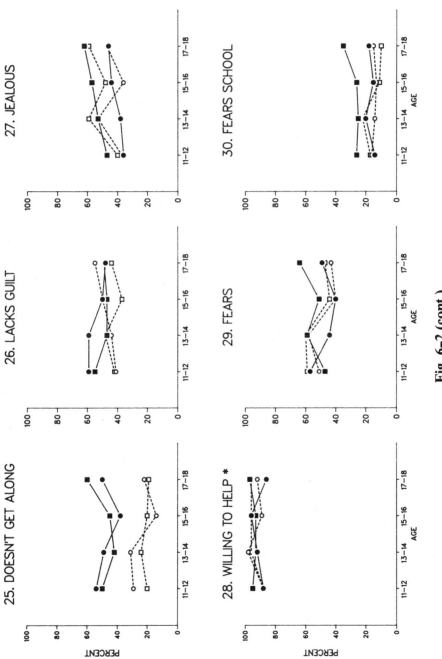

Fig. 6-2 (cont.).

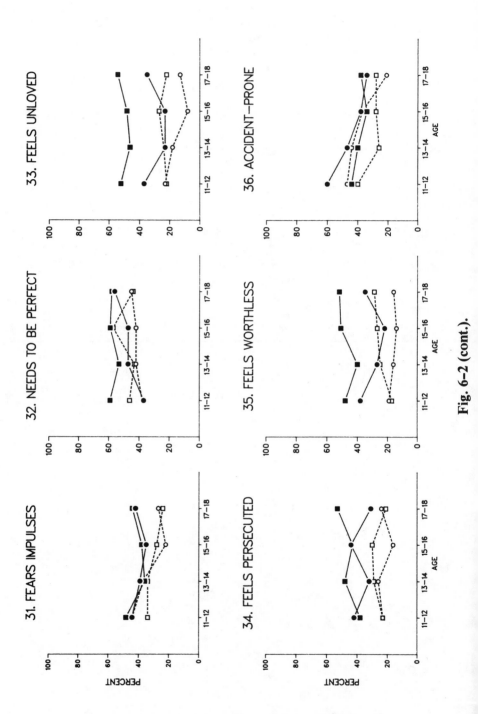

Fig. 6-2 (cont.).

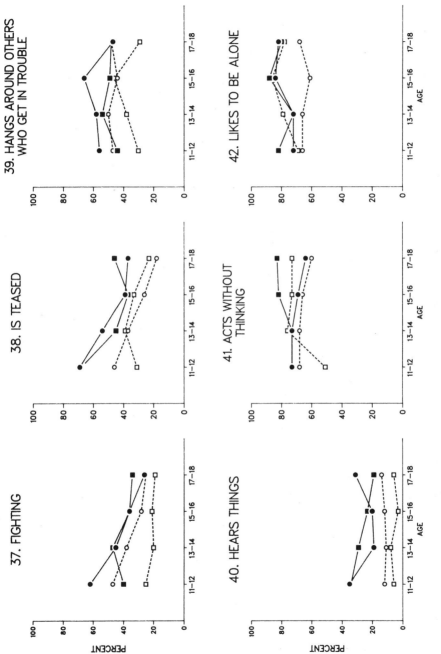

Fig. 6–2 (cont.).

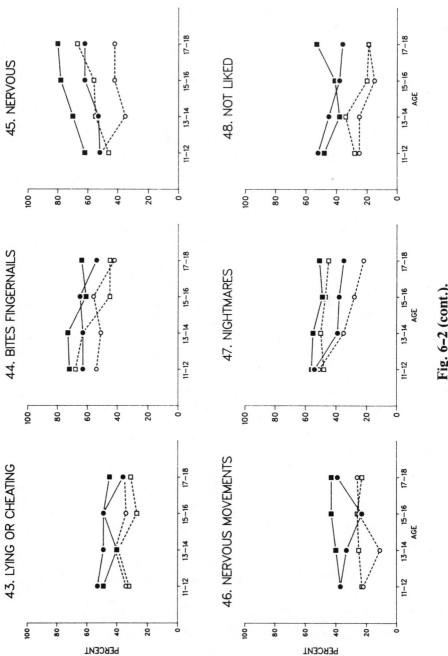

Fig. 6-2 (cont.).

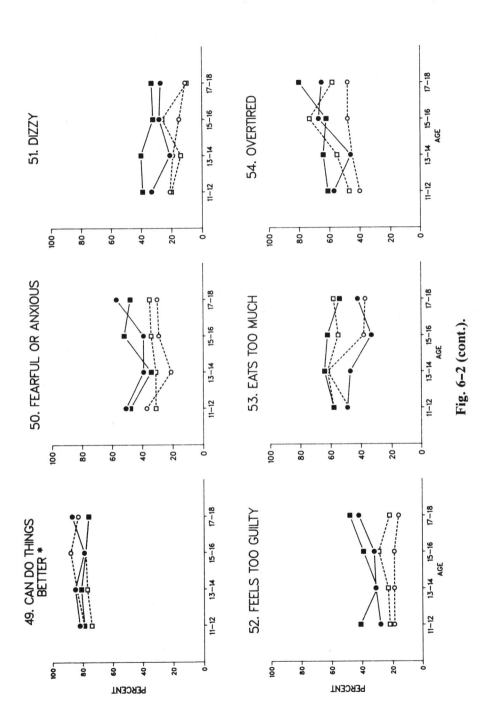

Fig. 6-2 (cont.).

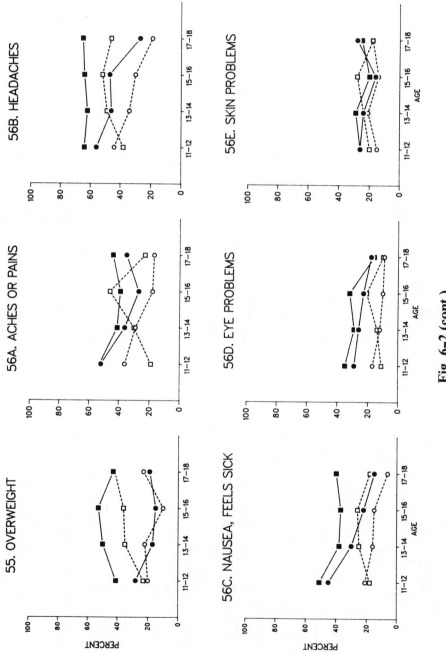

Fig. 6-2 (cont.).

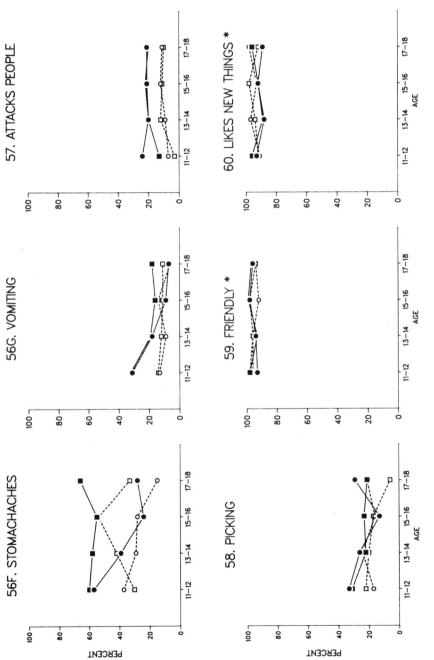

Fig. 6-2 (cont.).

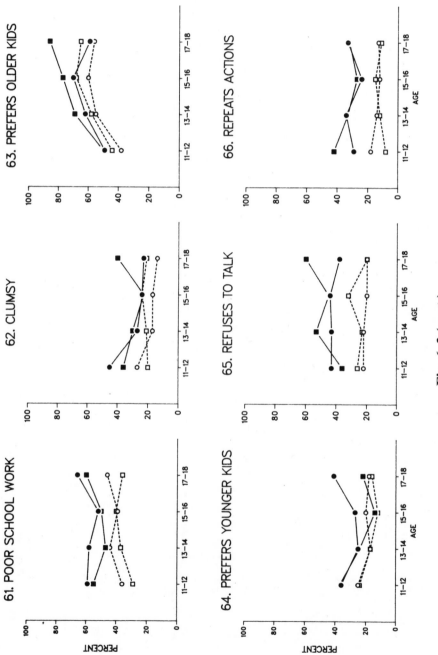

Fig. 6-2 (cont.).

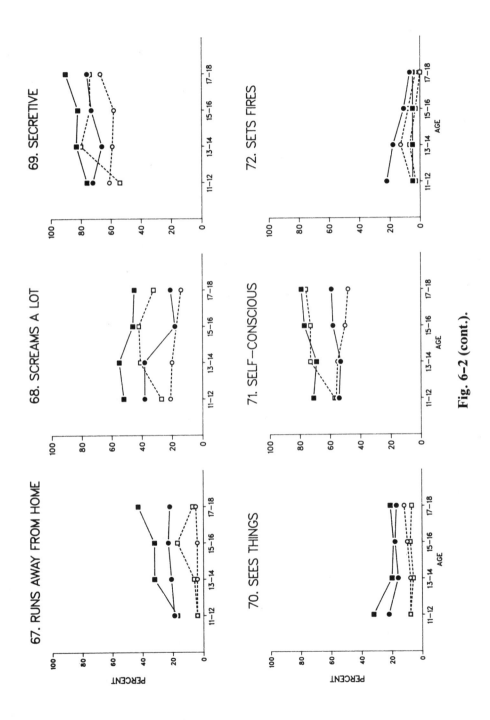

Fig. 6-2 (cont.).

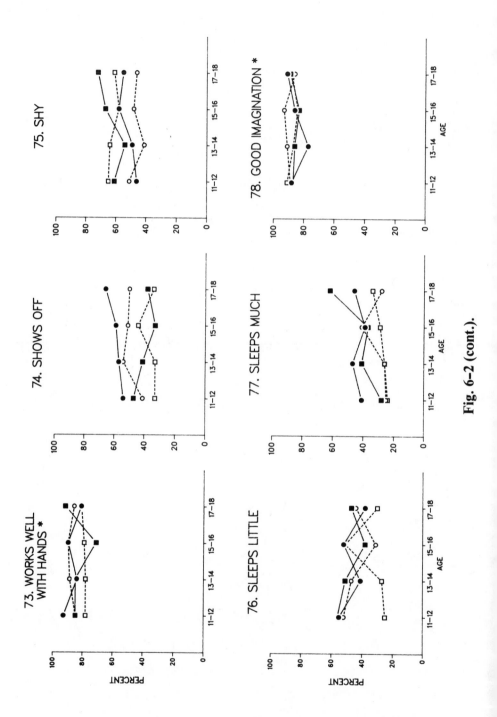

Fig. 6-2 (cont.).

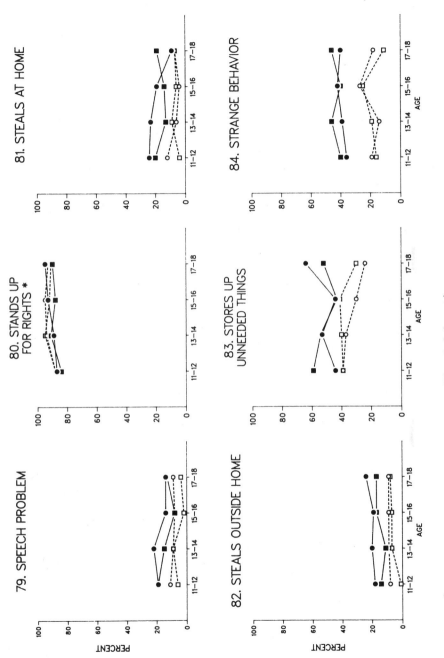

Fig. 6-2 (cont.).

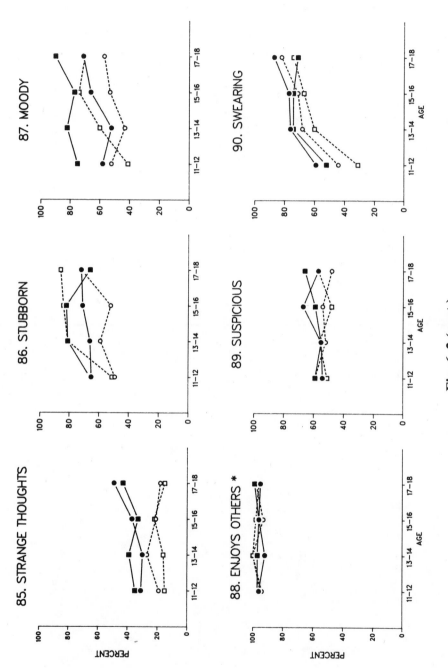

Fig. 6-2 (cont.).

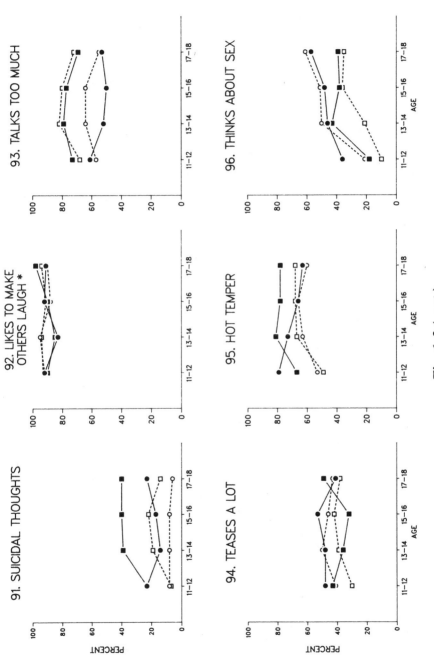

Fig. 6-2 (cont.).

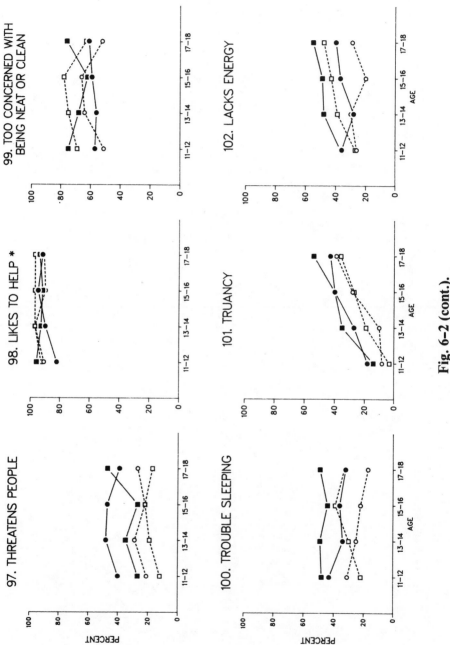

Fig. 6-2 (cont.).

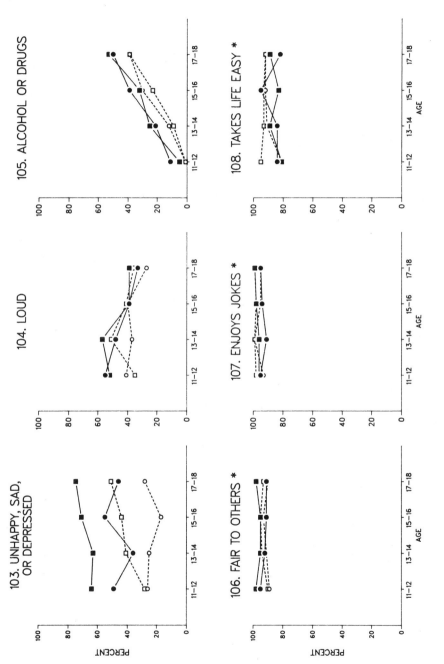

Fig. 6-2 (cont.).

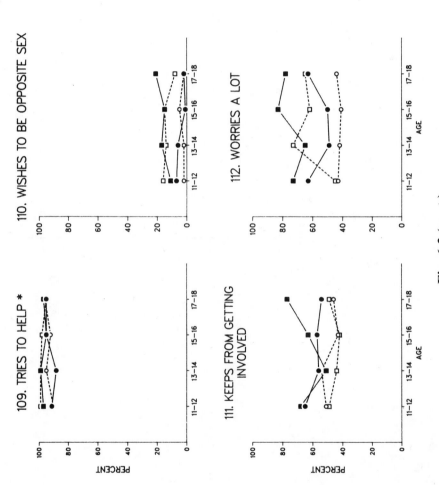

Fig. 6-2 (cont.).

SUMMARY

To determine which YSR items discriminate between adolescents referred for mental health services and demographically similar nonreferred adolescents, we analyzed scores on every item in relation to referral status, age, race, and SES.

Referred adolescents scored significantly ($p < .01$) lower on 8 of the 17 competence items, the Social scale, and the total competence score. However, referred adolescents reported liking to participate in significantly more sports and nonsports activities than nonreferred adolescents.

Referred adolescents scored significantly ($p < .01$) higher than nonreferred adolescents on 89 of the 102 specific problem items and the total problem score. The largest effects of referral status were on item 9. *I can't get my mind off certain thoughts* (20%), the total problem score (12%), and item 103. *Unhappy, sad, or depressed* (8%), which showed the strongest association with referral status in parent and teacher ratings on the CBCL and TRF.

Most referred and nonreferred adolescents endorsed the 16 socially desirable items, with significant but small tendencies for referred adolescents to score themselves lower on three of the items.

Sex showed more significant associations with item scores than did the other demographic variables. Most of the sex differences reflected higher scores on competence items for boys and higher scores on problem items for girls. The sex differences support the use of separate norms for boys and girls. However, the only sex differences exceeding Cohen's criteria for small effects were on item 14. *I cry a lot* (11%) and 55. *I am overweight* (6%), with girls scoring themselves higher on both.

Of the significant age differences on competence items, most involved higher scores for younger adolescents, but all were very small effects. Of the significant age differences on problem items, 15 involved higher scores for older adolescents, 15 higher scores for younger adolescents, and 5 were nonlinear effects. The only ones exceeding Cohen's criteria for small effects were 90. *I swear or use dirty language* (6%) and 105. *I use alcohol or drugs* (11%), with older adolescents scoring themselves higher on both.

There were no racial differences on competence items. Of the 16 problem items showing significant racial differences, whites scored themselves higher on 13, but none of the effects exceeded 1% of the variance. All 7 SES effects on competence items reflected higher scores for upper SES adolescents, while 21 of the 23 SES effects on problem items reflected higher scores for lower SES adolescents. None of the SES differences exceeded Cohen's criteria for small effects.

Figure 6-1 depicts mean scores on competence items and scales for adolescents grouped by age, sex, and referral status. Figure 6-2 similarly depicts the mean total problem scores and the percent of adolescents reporting each problem and socially desirable item. The percent obtaining scores of 1, 2, and the sum of these is listed in Appendix E. Each data point in Figures 6-1 and 6-2 and Appendix E is based on weighting scores to reflect samples that are 20% black and 80% white, with 1/3 lower, 1/3 middle, and 1/3 upper SES for the whites.

Chapter 7
Relations of the YSR to the CBCL and TRF

As we have stressed throughout this Manual, neither the YSR nor any other assessment procedure should be the sole criterion for judging adolescents' need for professional help. Our meta-analyses have shown low to moderate correlations between ratings of behavioral/emotional problems by different informants using many different instruments in different samples (Achenbach, McConaughy, & Howell, 1987). In this chapter, we will present correlations of the YSR with the CBCL and TRF in referred and nonreferred samples, as well as comparisons between mean problem scores obtained on the YSR and the other two instruments.

CORRELATIONS BETWEEN CORRESPONDING YSR AND CBCL SCALES

Table 7-1 presents Pearson correlations between YSR scores and corresponding CBCL scales for boys, while Table 7-2 presents the correlations for girls. Note that the correlations are based on similar YSR and CBCL items—albeit not identically worded—only for the following scales: Activities, Social, School (ratings for academic subjects only), and total problems (the 103 problem items that are similar on the YSR and CBCL). The remaining scores are based on sets of items that are similar enough to be summarized with similar labels on the two instruments, but the specific items differ considerably between some of the scales that have similar labels. The differences between items may therefore limit correlations more for these scales than for scores based on similar items.

As Tables 7-1 and 7-2 show, the mean of the YSR x CBCL correlations was .41 for boys and .45 for girls, computed for samples combining referred and nonreferred adolescents. For all four separate samples of boys and three of the four samples

Table 7-1
Correlations Between Corresponding YSR and
CBCL Scales for Boys

Scale	Referred x Either Parent	Nonreferred x Either Parent	Combined Ref. & Nonref.	Nonreferred x Mother [a]	x Father [a]
	N = 105	326	431	29	29
Activities	.26	.39	.36	.37	(.22)
Social	.38	.42	.47	.39	(.18)
School [b]	.72 [d]	.50 [e]	.59	.60	.66
Total Competence	.41	.43	.45	.54	.40
Somatic	.26	.28	.30	(−.06)	(.05)
Thought Disorder (Schizoid on CBCL)	.20	(.07)	.15	(.26)	(.23)
Delinquent	.44	.44	.49	(.09)	.51
Aggressive	.39	.33	.38	(.10)	(.22)
Internalizing	.37	.34	.42	(.29)	.43
Externalizing	.41	.38	.43	(.13)	.46
Total Problems [c]	.36	.31 [d]	.39 [d]	(.16 [d])	.48 [d]
Mean r	.37	.36	.41	.27	.36

Note. Correlations are for raw scale scores. All but those in parentheses are significant at $p < .05$.

[a] From V.S. Phares, B.E. Compas, & D.C. Howell, unpublished data. The nonreferred x mother and x father are adolescents whose mothers and fathers filled out separate CBCLs.

[b] YSR x CBCL ratings for academic performance (not the entire CBCL School scale).

[c] YSR problems x the 103 CBCL items that have counterparts on the YSR.

[d] YSR score > CBCL score for same items at $p < .05$.

[e] CBCL score > YSR score for same items at $p < .05$.

of girls, the highest correlation between adolescents and their parents was for ratings of performance in academic subjects, which ranged from .49 to .72. In the large normative samples of both sexes, parents rated academic performance significantly higher than their adolescents did, whereas the reverse was true

Table 7-2

**Correlations Between Corresponding YSR and
CBCL Scales for Girls**

Scale	Referred x Either Parent N = 61	Nonreferred x Either Parent 327	Combined Ref. & Nonref. 388	Nonreferred x Mother[a] 34	x Father[a] 34
Activities	.43	.48	.49	(.19)	.36
Social	.34	.49	.47	.49	.59
School[b]	.68	.57[e]	.62	.51	.49
Total Competence	.45	.54	.53	.49	.58
Somatic	(.22)	.22	.26	(.30)	.37
Depressed	.47	.20	.29	(−.10)	(.07)
Thought Disorder (Schizoid on CBCL)	.58	.23	.40	(.17)	(.32)
Delinquent	.66	.46	.55	(.30)	.44
Aggressive	.46	.35	.41	(.19)	(.28)
Internalizing	.49	.26	.38	(.03)	(.23)
Externalizing	.59	.41	.49	(.22)	(.33)
Total Problems[c]	.56[d]	.34[d]	.44[d]	(.32[d])	.43[d]
Mean r	.50	.39	.45	.27	.38

Note. Correlations are for raw scale scores. All but those in parentheses are significant at $p < .05$.
[a]From V.S. Phares, B.E. Compas, & D.C. Howell, unpublished data. The nonreferred x mother and x father are adolescents whose mothers and fathers filled out separate CBCLs.
[b]YSR x CBCL ratings for academic performance (not the entire CBCL School scale).
[c]YSR problems x the 103 CBCL items that have counterparts on the YSR.
[d]YSR score > CBCL score for same items at $p < .05$.
[e]CBCL score > YSR score for same items at $p < .05$.

for referred boys. There was not much consistency among the samples with respect to the scales showing the lowest YSR x CBCL correlations.

The correlation of .27 between CBCLs completed by mothers and YSRs completed by both their nonreferred sons and daughters approximates the mean of .25 found in our meta-analyses of parent-child correlations (Achenbach et al., 1987). However, the mean CBCL x YSR correlations for all the other groups exceeded this level, ranging up to .50 for ratings of referred girls by either parent. Except for mothers' ratings of their sons, the correlations were somewhat higher for Externalizing than Internalizing problems in all samples shown in Tables 7-1 and 7-2. Higher correlations for Externalizing than Internalizing problems were also found in our meta-analyses.

In the samples for which mothers and fathers completed separate CBCLs for their adolescents, YSR scores tended to correlate higher with fathers' CBCL ratings than with mothers' CBCL ratings. Although the size of the difference between the mean correlations was similar for both sexes (.36 versus .27 for boys, .38 versus .27 for girls), t tests showed that the difference was highly significant for girls at $p < .001$ but not significant for boys, owing to greater variance.

CORRELATIONS BETWEEN CORRESPONDING YSR AND TRF SCALES

Table 7-3 lists correlations between corresponding YSR and TRF scales. Because the overall similarity of the YSR to the TRF is less than to the CBCL, there are fewer corresponding scales. For the combined referred and nonreferred samples, the mean correlations were .43 for boys and .45 for girls, quite similar to the mean correlations of .41 and .45 found for the YSR x CBCL scales. No one scale showed consistently higher or lower correlations than the others, although the correlations were higher for Externalizing than for Internalizing, as is typically found.

Table 7-3
Correlations Between Corresponding YSR and TRF Scales

	Boys			Girls		
	Ref.	Nonref.[a]	Combined Ref. & Nonref.	Ref.	Nonref.[a]	Combined Ref. & Nonref.
Scale	N = 46	37	83	28	34	62
School	(.21)	—	—	.75	—	—
Depressed (girls only)	—	—	—	.63	(.03)	.59
Unpopular	(.11)	(.03)	(.19)	(.13)	(.23)	(.20)
Delinquent	—	—	—	(.32)	(.29)	.39
Aggressive	.57	.53	.53	(.22)	.34	.45
Internalizing	.27	(-.01)	.37	.40	(.10)	.47
Externalizing	.56	.55	.59	.43	.35	.56
Total Problems	.26[b]	.35[b]	.41[b]	.41[b]	(.08)[b]	.44[b]
Mean r	.35	.31	.43	.43	.21	.45

Note. Correlations are for raw scale scores. All but those in parentheses are are significant at $p < .05$.

[a]From V.S. Phares, B.E. Compas, & D.C. Howell, unpublished data. Ratings of school performance were not obtained for this sample and are therefore excluded from the combined samples as well.

[b]YSR score > TRF for same items at $p < .05$.

MEAN PROBLEM SCORES ON THE YSR, CBCL, AND TRF

Table 7-4 compares mean total problem scores for corresponding items on the YSR versus the CBCL and on the YSR versus the TRF. It is evident that nonreferred adolescents reported considerably more problems than either their parents or teachers, with all *t* tests for nonreferred adolescents showing significantly higher problem scores on the YSR than on the CBCL or TRF at $p < .01$. Mothers' CBCL problem scores did not differ significantly more from those of fathers for their sons, but mothers reported significantly more problems for their daughters than fathers did (mean problem scores 27.9 versus 21.0, $p < .01$ by t test). There was a correlation of .75 between parents' ratings, however, which indicates considerable agreement in the rank ordering of total problem scores.

Table 7-4
Mean Problem Scores for Referred and Nonreferred
Samples on Corresponding Items of
the YSR, CBCL, and TRF

		YSR			CBCL	
	N	Mean	SD		Mean	SD
Referred						
Boys	104	53.5	25.1	Either parent:	48.9	22.5
Girls	61	59.7[b]	28.3	Either parent:	44.3	27.1
Nonreferred						
Boys[a]	29	39.6[b]	18.8	Fathers:	24.2	15.7
				Mothers:	23.2	12.0
Girls[a]	34	43.9[b]	21.2	Fathers:	21.0	23.3
				Mothers:	27.9[c]	25.7
Boys	326	40.1[b]	21.2	Either parent:	24.9	19.7
Girls	327	44.0[b]	22.3	Either parent:	23.0	20.3
Referred					*TRF*	
Boys	46	49.6[b]	24.0		39.6	24.7
Girls	28	64.0[b]	27.0		28.1	20.2
Nonreferred						
Boys[a]	37	34.9[b]	17.0		16.2	16.6
Girls[a]	34	38.9[b]	16.5		6.4	9.4

Note. Comparisons between pairs of instruments are based on the problem items that are similar between the members of the pair: 103 similar items on the YSR and CBCL; 90 similar items on the YSR and TRF.
[a]From V.S. Phares, B.E. Compas, & D.C. Howell, unpublished data.
[b]YSR scores > CBCL or TRF scores at $p < .01$.
[c]Mothers' scores > fathers' scores at $p < .05$.

The YSR problem scores for referred boys did not differ significantly from their CBCL problem scores (53.5 versus 48.9). Although the referred boys' YSR problem scores were significantly higher than their TRF problem scores at $p < .05$, this difference was smaller (49.6 versus 39.6) than found for most of the other comparisons of YSR scores with CBCL and TRF scores. The referred girls' YSR scores were significantly higher than either their CBCL scores (59.7 versus 44.3) or their TRF scores (64.0 versus 28.1), both $p < .001$.

SUMMARY

For samples including referred and nonreferred adolescents, correlations between scores on corresponding scales of the YSR and CBCL averaged .41 for boys and .45 for girls. For corresponding scales of the YSR and TRF, the correlations averaged .43 for boys and .45 for girls. Although modest, the correlations of the YSR with the CBCL and TRF are considerably larger than those found in our meta-analyses of many instruments, where the mean r was .25 for parent x child ratings and .20 for teacher x pupil ratings. Despite statistically significant associations between YSR ratings and those by parents and teachers, it is nevertheless evident that adolescents' self-reports are not substitutes for reports by adults who know them, nor vice versa. It is also evident that adolescents generally report more problems than their parents or teachers, although there was no significant difference between YSR and CBCL total problem scores for referred boys.

Chapter 8
Practical and Research Applications of the YSR

To improve our understanding of adolescents and our ways of helping them, we have designed the YSR to serve both practical and research purposes. The YSR is intended to provide standardized self-reports in a form that is useful for practitioners needing to make decisions about particular adolescents and for researchers addressing more general questions. By providing an assessment procedure designed for both practice and research, we hope to help practitioners profit from research findings and researchers to focus on issues arising in practice.

This chapter is intended to guide users in applying the YSR to their own practical and research needs. The most basic function of the YSR is to obtain self-reports in a standardized fashion that facilitates comparison with self-reports by normative samples of adolescents, with self-reports at different points in time, and with parents' and teachers' judgments of the adolescents. The following sections outline the ways in which this function can be utilized.

APPLICATIONS IN MENTAL HEALTH CONTEXTS

The YSR can be used in mental health settings ranging from private practices to outpatient clinics, forensic clinics, acute care hospitals, group homes, and residential centers. To accumulate experience with the YSR in a particular setting and to insure a uniform baseline of clinical data from which to identify changes in individual adolescents over time, it is desirable to have the YSR completed at an early point in contacts with each referred adolescent. The precise point at which the YSR is completed and the conditions under which it is completed may vary between settings and between cases within a setting, as discussed in the following sections.

Clinical Intake

Most referrals of adolescents are initiated by adults, such as parents and teachers. Intake information comes mainly from adults, usually parents or parent surrogates. The CBCL is designed to obtain parents' descriptions of their children in a standardized format. In many settings, the CBCL can be obtained uniformly as part of the referral or intake process for virtually every case. The CBCL can be repeated at later points during and after an intervention to evaluate change as reported by parents.

When adolescents are brought for mental health services, they can be asked to fill out the YSR to obtain their views for comparison with their parents' CBCL, to provide a baseline for comparison with subsequent assessments, and to encourage expression of the adolescents' own concerns. Whereas the CBCL is typically completed by parents before their first clinical interview, the timing of the YSR depends more on individual circumstances. For most adolescents—especially those toward the upper end of the 11- to 18-year age range—the YSR can be completed before or at the initial contact, just as the CBCL is completed by parents before or at the initial contact. For adolescents who resist referral and deny needing help, one or two introductory clinical interviews may be required before they are cooperative enough to complete the YSR. On the other hand, some resistant adolescents are more willing to complete the YSR than to express themselves in interviews. Not only do their YSR responses provide information not obtainable via interview, but completing the YSR often encourages them to talk about themselves. In most situations, the YSR can be introduced as follows:

> "I (or we) would like you to fill out this form in order to obtain your views of your interests, feelings, and behavior."

The respondent should be assured of confidentiality, including confidentiality from parents. The clinician or someone else familiar with the YSR should be available to answer any questions the adolescent has while completing it. Questions should be answered in an objective and factual manner to help the adolescent understand the literal meaning of items, rather than to probe the adolescent's thoughts. If the YSR is administered orally, it should be done out of earshot of others. The completed YSR and the scored profile should not be accessible to unauthorized persons.

Clinical Interviewing

After the YSR has been completed and scored, it can help to guide clinical interviewing. Adolescents may spontaneously wish to discuss their responses or begin talking about issues broached on the YSR, such as suicidal ideation, strange thoughts, sexual identity problems, or feelings of rejection. The clinician may wish to ask for clarification of certain items that the adolescent reports, especially such items as *9. I can't get my mind off certain thoughts; 40. I hear things that nobody else seems able to hear; 66. I repeat certain actions over and over; 70. I see things that nobody else seems able to see; 84. I do things other people think are strange;* and *85. I have thoughts that other people would think are strange.* Comments written by adolescents in the spaces beside items and in the spaces provided on pages 2 and 4 often help to explain their responses and provide material to be explored in clinical interviews.

After obtaining clarification of the adolescent's responses, the clinician can use the items of greatest concern and the profile scales showing the most deviance as foci for interviewing about the history and context of the problems. Profile scales found to be well below the clinical cutoff can provide a basis for reassurance that concerns in these areas are within the normal range. The competence portion of the profile can also be used to identify areas in which adolescents report competencies on a par with those of their agemates versus areas that should be targeted for improvement.

As clinical contacts progress, the adolescent can be asked to complete the YSR again in order to assess changes in self-reported feelings and behaviors. Repeat YSRs can be used as a continuing guide for clinical interviews, including discussion of how the adolescent feels about changes that are or are not occurring. At each administration of the YSR, it can also be compared with other types of data in order to coordinate findings from different perspectives, as discussed next.

Multiaxial Assessment

Although the YSR can be used alone, it is based on the assumption that no single source of data provides a complete picture of adolescents' functioning. The YSR is therefore viewed as one component of an approach to assessment that includes data from multiple sources, such as parents, teachers, standardized tests, physical assessment, direct observations, and clinical interviews. We call this approach *multiaxial assessment* to emphasize that several sources of data can each make different contributions to assessment.

When discrepancies are found between different sources, this does not necessarily mean that one is wrong and another is right, or that one source should take precedence over another. Nor does it mean that multiple sources of data must all converge on a single diagnostic construct. On the contrary, different sources of data may validly reveal different facets of an adolescent's functioning, each of which deserves attention when evaluating needs for help, planning interventions, and evaluating outcomes.

Elsewhere, we have presented a conceptual model for multiaxial assessment (Achenbach, 1985) and have illustrated its application in a variety of cases ranging from preschoolers to adolescents (Achenbach & McConaughy, 1987). As applied to assessment of adolescents, our model includes the following five axes:

> **Axis I—Parent Data.** Standardized ratings of the adolescent by parents, as on the CBCL; history of the adolescent's development, problems, competencies, and interests as reported by the parents; interviews with parents; workability of parents for various potential interventions.
>
> **Axis II—Teacher Data.** Standardized ratings of the adolescent by teachers, such as on the TRF; other teacher data, such as report cards, comments in school records, and

interviews with teachers; workability of teachers for various potential interventions.

Axis III—Cognitive Assessment. Ability tests, such as the WISC-R and WAIS-R; achievement tests; tests of perceptual-motor and speech-language functioning.

Axis IV—Physical Assessment. Height and weight; physical abnormalities and handicaps; medical and neurological examinations.

Axis V—Direct Assessment of the Adolescent. Standardized self-ratings paralleling parent and teacher ratings, as on the YSR; clinical interview; direct observations in customary environments such as school, recorded with instruments such as the Direct Observation Form (DOF) of the Child Behavior Checklist; self-concept measures; personality tests; workability for various potential interventions.

Table 8-1 summarizes the components of the multiaxial model in abbreviated form as it applies to the 11- to 18-year age range. The model provides guidelines rather than rigid prescriptions that must be precisely followed in all cases. Additional assessment procedures—such as sociometrics and family assessment—can be added to those listed in Table 8-1, if desired. We will illustrate application of the multiaxial model to an adolescent case involving the YSR later in the chapter.

Planning Interventions

The interventions to be considered in a particular case depend on many factors. Examples include the reasons for referral; who is concerned about the adolescent's functioning; the family and school situation; the type of mental health service to which the adolescent is referred; and the adolescent's view of his or her own problems.

The YSR can be especially helpful in identifying ways in which adolescents' views of themselves differ from or resemble others' views of them. If an adolescent receives scores in the clinical range on the CBCL and TRF but reports few problems

Table 8-1
Examples of Multiaxial Assessment of Adolescents

Axis I Parent Reports	Axis II Teacher Reports	Axis III Cognitive Assessment	Axis IV Physical Assessment	Axis V Direct Assessment
CBCL	TRF	WISC-R, WAIS-R	Height	YSR
Develop- mental history	School records	Achievement perceptual- motor,	Weight Medical	DOF Interview
Parent interview	Teacher interview	speech- language tests	Neuro- logical	Self- concept, personality tests

Note. Achenbach (1985) presents the conceptual framework for the multi-axial assessment model, while Achenbach and McConaughy (1987) illustrate applications ranging from the preschool period through adolescence.

on the YSR, for example, this suggests either a lack of awareness or a lack of candor regarding problems reported by others. Before choosing an intervention, it would be important to determine whether the adolescent is truly unaware of the problems, is aware of them but unwilling to take responsibility for them, or whether the other informants' reports are questionable.

If it becomes clear that the adolescent refuses to acknowledge problems that are substantiated by others, this would argue against interventions that presuppose spontaneous motivation to change oneself. If the adolescent and other informants agree in reporting externalizing problems, this would indicate that the adolescent's awareness of the problems is consistent with that of the other informants and that the adolescent may recognize the need for change.

If few internalizing problems are reported on the YSR, this suggests a lack of the personal discomfort usually needed to motivate talking therapies, but behavioral or milieu approaches may be feasible. Adolescents who obtain scores in the clinical range on the internalizing scales, on the other hand, may be better candidates for therapies that capitalize on feelings of discomfort with oneself.

Beside aiding in the choice of a general therapeutic approach, the YSR can help in selecting specific targets for change. This can be done by discussing with the adolescent the specific problems reported on the YSR that cause the most distress. It can also be done at the level of syndrome scale scores by targeting treatment on the syndromal areas that show the greatest deviance, such as those indicated by the Depressed, Somatic Complaints, Thought Disorder, Unpopular, Self-Destructive/Identity Problems, Aggressive, or Delinquent scales. Problem areas that are substantiated by other assessment procedures but are not acknowledged by the adolescent may be targeted for bringing to the adolescent's attention.

Reassessments During and After Treatment

After an intervention begins, the YSR can be readministered periodically to track changes as they are seen by the adolescent. It is important to track changes across all problem areas, rather than reassessing only those areas that were targeted for change. Even though an adolescent was initially most deviant on the Aggressive scale of the YSR, for example, it is possible that a reduction of overt aggression may be followed by failure to improve or worsening in other areas, such as indicated by the Depressed scale. Reassessments should therefore be used to provide continuing guidance for helping the adolescent, rather than merely determining whether the targeted problems have improved.

The YSR, CBCL, and TRF can all be used for post-treatment assessments to determine outcomes. It is especially useful to plan reassessments at uniform intervals for all cases in a caseload. For example, if all adolescents are scheduled to complete the YSR at intake and again at 6-month intervals thereafter, it is possible to accumulate data on the typical course of changes for adolescents in that caseload. This can reveal the proportion who show major improvements versus no change or worsening.

It can also be used to determine whether there are particular problems, types of adolescents, or family situations, for example, that show exceptionally good versus poor outcomes with particular interventions.

If parents and teachers are available, the CBCL and TRF can be readministered at the same intervals to determine whether similar patterns of change are reported by the different informants. In some cases, favorable changes reported on the YSR may not be borne out by the CBCL or TRF, or vice versa. Such findings would suggest a need for altering interventions to facilitate improvement in the areas that failed to improve.

Case Example

The precise point at which the YSR is obtained in a clinical evaluation and the additional assessment procedures used depend on the nature of the clinical setting and the particular case. Figure 8-1 schematically depicts a sequence applicable to diverse clinical settings. The specific procedures may vary from case to case, with some of the listed procedures being omitted or used in different order, while procedures not listed in Figure 8-1 are also used. A family therapist, for example, may prefer to conduct all interviews conjointly with parents and the adolescent, rather than separately. If an adolescent is not attending school, the TRF and DOF would not be used. Psychological tests would not be administered if adequate test data were already available.

The following case illustrates the integration of the YSR with other procedures according to the general sequence depicted in Figure 8-1. To highlight the overall assessment model, we have omitted many clinical details, discussion of etiological factors, and consideration of alternative procedures.

> **Referral and Intake Assessment.** Ginny, a 16-year-old 10th grader, was brought to a mental health clinic by her parents after a brief hospitalization for an overdose of aspirin.
>
> Ginny had previously threatened suicide, but this was her first attempt. She had left a suicide

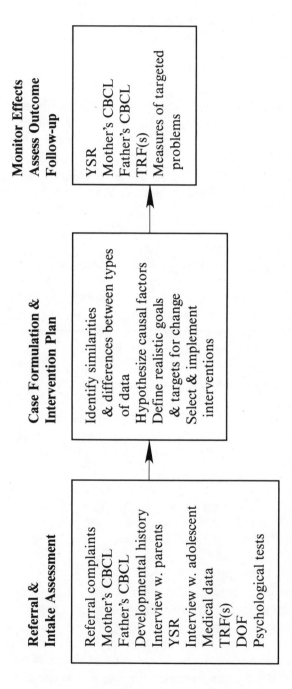

Referral &
Intake Assessment

Referral complaints
Mother's CBCL
Father's CBCL
Developmental history
Interview w. parents
YSR
Interview w. adolescent
Medical data
TRF(s)
DOF
Psychological tests

Case Formulation &
Intervention Plan

Identify similarities
  & differences between types
  of data
Hypothesize causal factors
Define realistic goals
  & targets for change
Select & implement
  interventions

Monitor Effects
Assess Outcome
Follow-up

YSR
Mother's CBCL
Father's CBCL
TRF(s)
Measures of targeted
  problems

Fig. 8-1. Schematic sequence for assessment of adolescents referred for mental health services

note where her mother found it after she had ingested about 25 aspirin. She was taken to a hospital where her stomach was pumped and she remained overnight for observation. Her attending physician referred her to the local mental health clinic, where her parents brought her the following day.

As part of the clinic's routine intake procedure, both parents were asked to complete separate CBCLs, while Ginny was asked to fill out the YSR. They were assured of confidentiality and were asked to fill out the forms to reflect their own views, without consulting each other. While the CBCLs and YSR were being scored on a micro-computer, the parents completed the clinic's intake information form, which requested a developmental history and other background information. The completed CBCLs and YSRs and their scored profiles were given to the clinician who interviewed Ginny, followed by her parents, and then all three together.

Ginny's YSR yielded a total competence score of 12.0, which is equivalent to a T score of 40, falling at approximately the 16th percentile for 11- to 18-year-old girls. Both her Activities and Social scale scores were at the low end of the normal range. On item V, regarding close friends, Ginny reported having only one friend and having less than one contact per week with that friend. Her mean School Performance score was 1.5, reflecting two ratings of below average and two ratings of average for her performance in academic subjects. In the space on page 2 for describing school concerns and problems, she wrote "I used to like school, but now I hate going there at all."

On the YSR problem items, Ginny's total score was 90, which was well above the 89th percentile score of 70 that marks the top of the YSR normal range. As Figure 8-2 shows, her scores on the

Somatic Complaints and Unpopular scales were in the clinical range, while her score on the Depressed scale was on the border between the normal and clinical range. Her scores on the Thought Disorder, Aggressive, and Delinquent scales were all within the normal range.

On the CBCL competence scales, both parents' ratings were in general agreement with Ginny's, indicating activities, social, and school functioning toward the low end of the normal range. On the CBCL problem scales, ratings by Ginny's mother were well up in the clinical range on the Anxious-Obsessive, Somatic Complaints, and Depressed Withdrawal scales, but in the normal range on the remaining five scales. Ratings by Ginny's father were in the clinical range only on the Depressed Withdrawal scale. The total problem scores of 69 on the mother's CBCL and 60 on the father's CBCL were both well above the 90th percentile score of 37 that marks the top of the CBCL normal range for 12-16-year-old girls.

Interviews with Ginny and her parents indicated that school was a major focus of her problems. Several months earlier, the family moved to an urban area where Ginny entered a much larger and more diverse high school than in the small town where they previously resided. She had previously obtained good grades with little effort and had neighborhood friends with whom she went to school. In the new school, by contrast, she found it harder to get good grades and had not made new friends. The one close friend she indicated on the YSR lived in the town where the family had previously resided.

Because school was such an important issue and because the Unpopular scale showed the greatest deviance on her YSR profile, Ginny and her parents were asked for permission to obtain TRFs from her teachers. They granted permission to

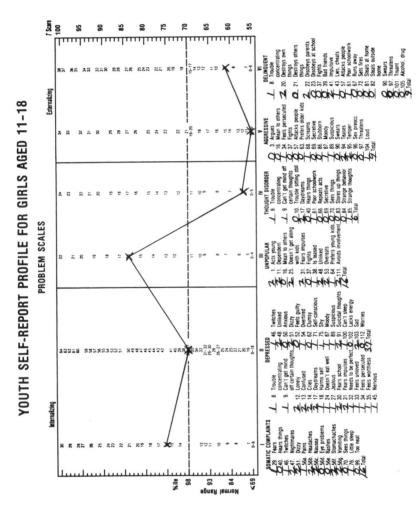

Fig. 8-2 Problem scales of a YSR profile completed for 16-year-old Ginny.

obtain TRFs from Ginny's math and history teachers who, they felt, were the only ones who knew her well enough to be helpful. Neither teacher knew about Ginny's suicide attempt.

The TRF completed by Ginny's history teacher yielded academic performance, adaptive functioning, and total problem scores in the normal range. Only the Immature scale was close to the clinical range, with a score just below the 98th percentile cutoff. The TRF completed by Ginny's math teacher showed academic performance and adaptive functioning at the low end of the normal range, but a total problem score of 52, which was above the 89th percentile score of 42 that marks the top of the TRF normal range for 12-16-year-old girls. The Immature scale scored from the math teacher's TRF was on the border between the normal and clinical range. However, the Inattentive and Social Withdrawal scales scored from the math teacher's TRF were both in the clinical range.

The comments written by the teachers on the TRF indicated that Ginny appeared to be an average though somewhat immature student in history, but was having problems in math that her teacher thought reflected inattention and lack of motivation. Neither teacher indicated any suicidal tendencies.

Test data from school records indicated that Ginny had obtained group IQ test scores ranging from 111 to 119 and achievement test scores in the average range. Because there was no reason to doubt these measures of her ability and achievement, cognitive testing was not done as part of the clinical evaluation. The medical work-up while she was in the hospital revealed no physical problems beside aftereffects of the overdose of aspirin.

Formulation and Intervention. The low score on the YSR Thought Disorder scale and the lack of any other evidence for poor reality testing or strange behavior on the CBCLs and TRFs indicated that psychotic tendencies were unlikely to be involved in Ginny's suicide attempt. Although her parents' CBCLs yielded scores in the clinical range on the Depressed Withdrawal scale, both scores were only moderately elevated. Ginny's score on the YSR Depressed scale was just above the border between the normal and clinical range, but her score was much higher on the YSR Unpopular scale. Neither teacher reported enough problems on the TRF Depressed scale to put it in the clinical range. Although Ginny was not a very happy girl, extreme depression did not appear to account for her suicide attempt.

A comparison of the profiles obtained from Ginny's YSR, her parents' CBCLs, and her teachers' TRFs indicated that her severest problems concerned feelings of rejection by peers, as manifest in her high score on the Unpopular scale of the YSR. Her teachers also reported some problems in peer relations, but not an exceptional concentration of problems in the area of unpopularity. Instead, her history teacher reported problems just below the clinical cutoff on the Immature scale, whereas her math teacher reported somewhat more problems of a similar nature, plus problems on the Social Withdrawal and Inattentive scales that were interfering with her progress in math. Her father's CBCL reflected mainly problems on the Depressed Withdrawal scale that were evident in his presence, whereas her mother's CBCL reflected additional problems of somatic complaints and anxiety about school, feelings of worthlessness, and loneliness that Ginny expressed to her.

Although most of Ginny's problems might be considered reactive to the family's move and her new school environment, the history obtained from her parents indicated that she had milder versions of similar problems where they had previously lived. Family tensions had also increased after the move, because of the demands of the father's new job. The TRF ratings suggested that Ginny was not actively rejected by peers, but that she was socially immature and reacted to new challenges—such as the math curriculum—with inattention and withdrawal.

Although her family's move and new school were not the only causes of Ginny's problems, they were the main foci of her concerns. Because her social and educational development was being impeded, it was decided to capitalize on her distress about peer relations to motivate the acquisition of new skills needed to advance her social and academic development. Her therapist met with her for five weekly sessions in which risks of suicide were evaluated and a plan for participation in a social skills group lead by another therapist was explored.

Because the risk of suicide seemed minimal, the individual therapy sessions were reduced to once a month for the next four months while Ginny attended the social skills group. The group was composed of adolescents who were having social and academic problems related to anxiety, feelings of rejection, poor peer relations, and the pressures of large urban schools. Several group members had made suicide attempts and most had at least contemplated suicide. The emphasis was on understanding that peers have similar problems, that such problems can be brought into the open, and that there are ways of overcoming them.

Outcome Assessment. A month after the social skills group ended, Ginny's therapist asked her to complete the YSR again, while both parents completed CBCLs. Her math and history teachers, who did not know of her social skills group attendance, completed TRFs. The YSR profile showed a substantial drop on the Unpopular scale, which was now at the 93rd percentile of the normal range. The Depressed scale also dropped from the 98th percentile to the 84th, while the Somatic Complaints scale dropped from the clinical range to the 98th percentile cutoff. The YSR total problem score dropped from 90 to 69, which is just below the clinical cutoff of 70. The CBCLs completed by both parents also showed decreases in total problem scores to the high normal range, as did the TRF completed by the math teacher. The scores on the TRF completed by the history teacher remained in the normal range.

Ginny had made some friends, accepted her new school situation, and seemed better able to cope actively with problems. She now denied contemplating suicide, but her therapist asked her and her parents to call if new problems arose. A follow-up six months later showed all CBCL and YSR problem scales in the normal range, although the YSR Somatic Complaints scale remained at the 98th percentile cutoff, reflecting Ginny's long-standing tendency to react somatically to minor stress.

SCHOOL SETTINGS

As illustrated in the preceding case, referrals of adolescents for mental health services often involve school-related problems and assessment data. The YSR can also be used for assessment and services within school systems.

Mandates for schools to provide special services—such as Public Law 94-142, the Education of All Handicapped Children Act—require systematic documentation of needs on which to base special services. As detailed elsewhere (Achenbach & Edelbrock, 1986; Achenbach & McConaughy, 1987), the TRF can provide a cornerstone for most school-based assessments. Even if pupils are learning disabled (LD), educable mentally retarded (EMR), or physically handicapped, the TRF can document behavioral/emotional problems and adaptive characteristics that are important in planning and evaluating services for these pupils. If LD, EMR, and handicapped pupils have a mental age of at least 10 years, the YSR can document their own perceptions of their problems and competencies for use in planning and evaluating school-based services.

For pupils whose eligibility for special services is not so obvious, the YSR, TRF, CBCL, and DOF can contribute to the determination of eligibility. These instruments can play an especially crucial role in documenting eligibility for services to the seriously emotionally disturbed (SED) and for determining whether pupils are more appropriately considered SED or LD. Table 8-2 outlines PL94-142 criteria for SED that can be assessed in terms of the YSR, TRF, CBCL, and DOF.

If referred pupils do not show deviance on any of the scales relevant to the SED criteria, they are unlikely to qualify for SED services under most interpretations of PL94-142. If they do show deviance on scales relevant to the SED criteria and also show evidence of a learning disability, then services should be planned to address both types of problems. It should be remembered that categories such as SED and LD are designed for administrative purposes to determine eligibility for special education services. The categories are not mutually exclusive, and most pupils do not fall neatly into only one category. Instead, pupils who have emotional problems often have learning problems and vice versa. Beside aiding in the administrative determination of eligibility for services, the YSR, TRF, CBCL, and DOF should therefore be used to tailor services to the pupil's specific needs, regardless of the administrative category of services. The following case illustrates the use of the YSR, TRF, CBCL, and DOF in school-based assessment to determine eligibility for services.

Table 8-2
Applications of Empirically-Based Assessment to PL 94-142 Criteria for Serious Emotional Disturbance

PL 94-142 Components of SED	CBCL	TRF	YSR	DOF
Inability to learn	—	Inattentive	—	On task Withdrawn- Inattentive
Inability to build or maintain relationships	Social Withdrawal Hostile Withdrawal	Social Withdrawal Unpopular	Unpopular	—
Inappropriate types of behavior or feelings	Schizoid Schizoid-Anxious Schizoid-Obsessive Obsessive-Compulsive Aggressive Hyperactive	Self-Destructive Obsessive- Compulsive Nervous-Overactive Aggressive	Thought Disorder Self-Destructive/ Identity Problems Aggressive	Nervous-Obsessive Attention- Demanding Aggressive Hyperactive
General pervasive mood of unhappiness	Depressed Depressed- Withdrawal	Depressed	Depressed	Depressed

Table 8-2 (Cont'd)
Applications of Empirically-Based Assessment to PL 94-142 Criteria for Serious Emotional Disturbance

PL 94-142 Components of SED	CBCL	TRF	YSR	DOF
Tendency to develop physical symptoms or fears	Somatic Complaints Schizoid-Anxious Anxious-Obsessive	Anxious	Somatic Complaints	—
Schizophrenic	Schizoid	—	Thought Disorder	—
Long period of time	Follow-up evaluations	Follow-up evaluations	Follow-up evaluations	Follow-up evaluations
Marked degree	Total, Internalizing, or Externalizing scores > 90th %tile	Total, Internalizing, or Externalizing scores > 89th %tile	Total, Internalizing, or Externalizing scores > 89th %tile	Total score > 93rd %tile
	Narrow-band scores > 98th %tile	Narrow-band scores > 98th %tile	Narrow-band scores > 98th %tile	Narrow-band scores > 98th %tile
Adversely affects educational performance	School scale < 2nd %tile	School performance < 2nd %tile Adaptive functioning < 13th %tile	—	—

Case Example

Referral. Allen, a 12-year-old seventh grader, was referred to the school psychologist by his English teacher after a temper outburst in which he started hitting two other boys in class. The outburst was evidently provoked by some subtle teasing, but the teacher had been concerned for several months about Allen's oversensitivity to criticism, his inattention, and poor achievement.

Allen's cumulative record showed a longstanding pattern of marginal grades and achievement test scores in the low average range, somewhat below his IQ test scores, which were generally around 100. His record also contained occasional comments about inattention and immaturity, but no evidence of serious behavior problems.

Assessment. As part of the referral procedure, Allen's English teacher was asked to complete the TRF. When scored on the TRF profile, her ratings indicated school performance and adaptive characteristics ranging between the 2nd and 10th percentiles. The total TRF problem score of 83 was well above the clinical cutoff score of 56 for 12-16-year-old boys. The narrow-band Inattentive and Aggressive scales were both in the clinical range, while the Unpopular and Social Withdrawal scales were near the clinical cutoff. It was thus clear that the English teacher was reporting enough problems to warrant further evaluation and determination of eligibility for special services.

Allen's mother, who was a single parent, granted permission for a complete evaluation and agreed to fill out the CBCL. Allen's other teachers were asked to complete TRFs, and the school psychologist observed Allen and two comparison boys in three classes, using the DOF.

Scores on the TRFs ranged from the normal range for ratings by a science teacher who indicated that he did not know Allen well, to a total score of 90 from a social studies teacher who reported more problems on the Unpopular and Social Withdrawal scales than the English teacher had.

The school psychologist observed Allen and two other boys for 10 minutes each in three classes. Allen showed more problems than the other boys during the observation sessions (mean score = 8.5 versus 1.0 for the mean of the two comparison boys), and was on task much less of the time (39% versus 93% for the mean of the two comparison boys). Allen's total DOF problem score was above the clinical cutoff. The psychologist did not observe much aggressive behavior, but Allen's scores on the Withdrawn-Inattentive and Depressed scales of the DOF were above the clinical cutoff.

When interviewed by the school psychologist, Allen gave uninformative, monosyllabic replies to questions about his temper outburst. Owing to doubts about Allen's reading skills, the psychologist handed him a copy of the YSR and said he would read the items aloud. After the first few items, Allen began answering the questions without waiting for them to be read, indicating that his reading skills were adequate for the YSR. He was then allowed to complete the rest of the YSR on his own. The YSR profile showed that Allen acknowledged enough aggressive behavior like that reported by his English teacher to yield a score on the Aggressive scale in the clinical range. However, he also reported enough problems on the Depressed and Unpopular scales to put both of them in the clinical range as well.

On the CBCL, Allen's mother reported few activities or social contacts and mediocre school functioning, resulting in a total competence score in the clinical range. On the problem portion of the CBCL profile, she reported enough problems of the Uncommunicative, Hostile Withdrawal, and

Aggressive scales to put all of them in the clinical range. In an interview with the school psychologist, she indicated that Allen had always been somewhat shy and uncommunicative, but that, since his father had left the family a year ago, he had become moody, hostile, and angry.

Determination of Eligibility. In terms of the PL94-142 criteria listed in Table 8-2, Allen would not have been eligible for special services on the basis of learning disabilities or on the basis of the referral complaints of aggressive behavior, since his state's interpretation of PL94-142 did not include aggression as a basis for SED eligibility. However, his TRF, DOF, YSR, and CBCL total problem scores in the clinical range and his low school scale scores were evidence for emotional disturbance of a marked degree that adversely affected his educational performance. SED eligibility was supported by his own reports of problems sufficient to yield YSR Depressed and Unpopular scores in the clinical range, corroborated by the psychologist's DOF ratings and scores in the clinical range for withdrawal on TRFs from two teachers and the CBCL from his mother. Taken together, these findings supported a determination that Allen met the PL94-142 criteria for "inability to build or maintain relationships" and "general pervasive mood of unhappiness."

Beside being used to determine eligibility, the data obtained with the YSR, TRF, CBCL, and DOF can be used to select specific targets for change through special educational services. The instruments can then be readministered to monitor change and to fulfill requirements for periodic re-evaluation of pupils receiving special educational services. If an adolescent's needs cannot be met within the school system, the data obtained with our instruments can be used to support referral for outside services, such as residential treatment.

Confidentiality in School Settings

Confidential data present special problems in schools. Most schools maintain a cumulative record on every pupil that includes grades, teachers' comments, and group test scores. Such records are usually available to teachers, but may often be accessible to others as well, even including pupils who help in school offices. Because pupils filling out the YSR should be assured of confidentiality, their responses and their YSR profiles should not be accessible to unauthorized people. The following safeguards of confidentiality should be observed:

1. Unless YSRs are to be completed anonymously for group studies or needs assessments, parental permission should be obtained for individual evaluations in which the YSR is employed.

2. The YSR should be administered to the pupil by a professional, such as a school psychologist, who is trained in assessment of adolescent psychopathology. The professional should tell the pupil the reason for the assessment, assure confidentiality, answer the pupil's questions, and administer the YSR orally if reading is a problem. Although pupils whose reading skills are adequate can fill out the YSR alone, the professional should remain available to answer questions.

3. Adolescents respond to the YSR not only with self-ratings, but also with comments that are personally revealing. It is therefore essential that the YSR be scored only by people who will protect its confidentiality and that the completed YSR and scored profile not be left in cumulative records or in other locations where its confidentiality may be compromised. Instead, it should be protected in the same way as other highly confidential material, such as psychological test reports.

DIAGNOSTIC ISSUES

As discussed in the preceding sections, special educational services usually require justification according to administrative categories, such as those prescribed by PL94-142. Diagnostic classification systems, such as DSM-III-R (American Psychiatric Association, 1987), often serve an analogous function for purposes of third party reimbursement for services. Although the concept of diagnosis also implies comprehensive case formulations, the DSM-III-R categories of child/adolescent disorders do not constitute detailed formulations. Instead, they are defined largely by lists of descriptive features and rules specifying the number of features required to meet the criterion for each diagnosis.

The DSM criteria are conventions formulated by committees. These conventions are subject to change, as illustrated by the substantial changes from the DSM-III to the DSM-III-R categories of child/adolescent disorders and in the defining criteria for the categories that have survived. Although it is hoped that different causes will ultimately be found to underlie the different categories of disorders, it is not known whether the DSM child/adolescent categories actually reflect underlying differences.

Many adolescents manifest features of multiple DSM categories, rather than fitting neatly into single categories. It is therefore important to base help on accurate assessment of all their needs, instead of viewing them only in terms of diagnostic categories.

The instruments we have developed provide a differentiated picture of problems and competencies as they are seen from different perspectives, rather than forcing them into predetermined categories. Nevertheless, the empirically-based syndromes and scores are highly relevant to diagnostic classifications, as well as to more comprehensive diagnostic formulations. Several of the syndromes derived empirically from our instruments have approximate counterparts in the DSM-III-R, as summarized in Table 8-3. These relations concern similarities in descriptive features, although efforts to operationalize assessment of DSM diagnostic categories have also confirmed significant statistical associations with the empirically-derived syndromes (Edelbrock, 1984; Edelbrock, Costello, & Kessler, 1984). In making DSM diagnoses, scores in the clinical range on the empirically-derived scales would argue in favor of the corresponding DSM diagnoses listed in the left-hand column of Table 8-3.

RELATIONS OF THE YSR TO
OTHER PROBLEMS

Beside assessment of behavioral/emotional problems in relation to referrals for mental health and special educational services, the YSR can also be used in other contexts, such as the assessment of physically ill adolescents and assessment in forensic contexts, as described in the following sections.

Physical Illness and Handicaps

Adolescents who have a serious physical illness or handicap may have concomitant behavioral or emotional problems. Such adolescents may be restricted from activities that are important in their peer group, may be teased or ostracized, may be impeded in school work, and may suffer discomfort or anxiety because of their condition.

The CBCL, TRF, and DOF can be used to pinpoint specific ways in which the problems and competencies of such adolescents differ from those of normative samples of agemates, as seen by other people. This can be helpful in planning placements and in identifying areas in which an ill or handicapped adolescent may need special help in adapting to peer groups. The YSR can likewise be helpful in identifying emotional problems that may not be apparent to others. Adolescents often report more internalizing problems on the YSR than are reported by adults on the CBCL, TRF, or DOF. The internalizing problems reported by ill and handicapped adolescents may be especially useful for identifying the subjective concerns with which the adolescents need help in adapting to their physical conditions.

Table 8-3
Approximate Relations Between DSM-III-R and Empirically-Derived Syndromes

DSM-III-R	CBCL	TRF	YSR	DOF
Solitary Aggressive Conduct Disorder Oppositional Defiant Disorder	Aggressive	Aggressive	Aggressive	Aggressive
Group Delinquent Conduct Disorder	Delinquent	Delinquent	Delinquent	—
Attention Deficit-Hyperactivity Disorder	Hyperactive Nervous-Overactive	Inattentive	—	Hyperactive
Overanxious Disorder	Anxious-Obsessive Schizoid-Anxious	Anxious	—	Nervous-Obsessive

Table 8-3 (Cont'd)
Approximate Relations Between DSM-III-R and Empirically-Derived Syndromes

DSM-III-R	CBCL	TRF	YSR	DOF
Gender Identity Disorder for Males	Sex Problems (boys 4-5)	—	Self-Destructive/ Identity Problems (boys only)	—
Schizoid Personality	Social Withdrawal	Social Withdrawal	—	—
Schizotypal Personality Psychotic Disorders	Schizoid	—	Thought Disorder	—
Somatization Disorder	Somatic Complaints	—	Somatic Complaints	—
Obsessive-Compulsive Disorder	Obsessive-Compulsive	Obsessive-Compulsive	—	—
Major Depression Dysthymia	Depressed (girls only)	Depressed	Depressed	Depressed

For professionals who specialize in work with adolescents having a particular type of illness—such as diabetes or leukemia—or handicap—such as deafness or cerebral palsy—the YSR can be used to determine what concerns are most common among them and how these concerns differ from those of healthy adolescents. Once such concerns have been identified, therapy and support programs can be designed to focus on them. The efficacy of interventions can also be evaluated by readministering the YSR to assess reductions in these concerns.

Forensic Evaluations

The YSR can be used in a variety of court-related evaluations of adolescents. If an adolescent is accused of a crime, for example, courts often order evaluations to identify psychopathological and attitudinal factors that should be considered in the disposition of the case. Although accused adolescents are apt to deny aggressive and delinquent behavior on the YSR, the degree to which they acknowledge externalizing behaviors that are known to occur can serve as an index of their general candor.

The internalizing problems that adolescents report on the YSR can indicate whether they acknowledge enough inner discomfort—such as on the YSR Depressed scale—to be motivated for personal help. The Thought Disorder scale can indicate whether deficient reality testing may be involved, while the Unpopular scale can indicate feelings of rejection and alienation from peers. Specific items such as *18. I deliberately try to hurt or kill myself* and *91. I think about killing myself* are also important to examine for danger signs.

Another forensic use of the YSR is to evaluate adolescents after stressful experiences, such as sex abuse or family disruption. It can also be used in evaluations for placement decisions necessitated by custody disputes between parents and by state intervention to terminate parental rights. In these contexts, the YSR can aid in determining the degree and type of deviance expressed by the adolescent that should be considered in making dispositions and in evaluating reports by others about the adolescent. After a disposition has been made, such as placement with one of the parents, a foster home, or group home, the YSR and related instruments can be repeated periodically to monitor the adolescent's progress.

NEEDS ASSESSMENT

To determine the number of adolescents in a particular population who are likely to need help for behavioral/emotional problems, randomly-selected members of the population can be surveyed by having them complete the YSR anonymously. If the target adolescents can be reached through schools or other group settings, it may often be easier to have them all fill out YSRs at the same time, rather than arranging for randomly-selected subsamples to fill out YSRs. Obtaining YSRs for all members of a population also has the advantage of providing more accurate prevalence data than can be obtained from subsamples, especially for relatively uncommon problems.

YSR survey data can be used to determine the number of adolescents in the population who have total scores in the clinical range and the number who show marked deviance in particular areas, as indicated by high scores on particular syndrome scales, such as the Depressed or Aggressive scales. The proportion reporting specific problems—such as suicidal thoughts—can also be assessed by tabulating individual items. More differentiated analyses of the population can be made by determining the proportion of particular subgroups who show the highest rates of particular problems. If the target population consists of pupils in a school system, for example, comparisons can be made between boys and girls, different ethnic groups, younger versus older pupils, different schools, and students enrolled in different curricula, such as general versus college preparatory.

ACCOUNTABILITY FOR SERVICES

With increasing emphasis on accountability for services, it is important to document the types of problems for which services are rendered and the effects of the services on the problems. The YSR can contribute to accountability by having each adolescent complete it as part of the initial assessment process. The YSR and its profile can then become part of the adolescent's clinical record and can be used in conjunction with profiles from other informants in planning services. Thereafter, the YSR and other instruments can be readministered to monitor the progress and outcome of services. If improvement is not found, a change in the treatment should be considered. This general model can be employed for outpatient mental health services, inpatient and residential services, foster home placement, group homes, and school-based services.

Beside providing accountability for individual cases, the YSR can also provide accountability at the level of programs and variations within programs. The data obtained with the YSR across a defined period, such as a year, can be used to document the number of cases having particular types of problems, the degree of deviance in the cases served, the relations of particular problems to demographic variables, and the disposition of cases having particular problems. Such data are important for reporting clinical activities, justifying requests for funding, and program planning.

If a clinical service offers a variety of treatment modalities, the YSR can be used as one basis for assigning adolescents to the different modalities. Adolescents whose YSR profiles show deviance mainly on internalizing scales, for example, might be assigned to psychotherapy. Those who show deviance mainly on externalizing scales, by contrast, might be assigned to drug, behavioral, or milieu therapies. By reassessing the adolescents periodically, we can determine whether the outcomes for each group are favorable after receiving their respective treatment modalities.

We can also determine whether particular internalizing, mixed, or externalizing profile patterns, or particular problems or scale scores are related to especially poor outcomes. If so, this would indicate that better interventions need to be found for adolescents with these characteristics, either by assigning them to different treatment options than previously, by developing new interventions tailored more specifically to their needs, or by referring them to settings that might be more effective with them.

RESEARCH APPLICATIONS

In addition to collecting data for needs assessments and service accountability, the YSR can be used in a variety of more formal research endeavors. The topics listed here illustrate a few of the many possible research applications. The *Manual for the Child Behavior Checklist* (Achenbach & Edelbrock, 1983) provides a more extensive discussion of research possibilities for empirically-based assessment. To obtain an up-to-date bibliography of hundreds of studies that have used our empirically-based measures, the reader is advised to search the *Social Sciences Citation Index* for publications that cite T. M. Achenbach or C. S. Edelbrock.

Epidemiological Research

As discussed in Chapter 2, we obtained normative data for the YSR by sending interviewers to randomly selected homes in the Worcester, Massachusetts, metropolitan area. The procedures described in Chapter 2 for the YSR and in our *Society for Research in Child Development Monograph* (Achenbach & Edelbrock, 1981) for the CBCL illustrate a general approach to epidemiological research using our rating forms. The approach uses random sampling procedures to obtain representative samples of target individuals in a particular general population. Our objective was to obtain normative distributions of scores for every item and scale on our instruments.

Similar procedures can be used to compare prevalence rates and distributions of scores in different populations. An example is a comparison between CBCL item scores in our normative sample and in a sample of Dutch children obtained by similar procedures (Achenbach, Verhulst, Baron, & Akkerhuis, 1987). In this study, the prevalence rates of problems reported on the CBCL were found to be extremely similar despite the linguistic, cultural, and environmental differences between the United States and Holland.

The findings also indicated that the CBCL can be used to calibrate studies between the two countries. Although in this case, the findings were very similar for parent-reported problems between two populations, epidemiological studies of prevalence rates might find greater differences between problems reported on the YSR. Work is currently under way to compare YSR scores for American and Dutch adolescents, but similar studies are worth doing to compare other nationalities and various subgroups within a country or area. Particular ethnic groups or groups thought to be at high risk for certain problems can be studied by similar epidemiologic methods. The YSR and other empirically-based instruments can also be used in conjunction with other types of epidemiological assessment procedures— such as clinical interviews—to compare the prevalence rates for particular problems assessed by different methods.

Etiological Research

Grouping by YSR Similarities. One way to use the YSR in research on the causes of disorders is to group adolescents according to similarities in scale scores or profile patterns. The groups thus formed can then be compared on hypothesized etiological factors to determine whether the differences in self-reported problems reflect different etiologies. The following are examples of ways in which the YSR can be used to group adolescents in order to identify possible etiological differences:

1. Grouping adolescents who have a high score on a particular scale—such as the Depressed scale—for comparison with adolescents who have low scores on that scale.

2. Grouping adolescents whose highest score is on one scale—such as the Thought Disorder scale—for comparison with those whose highest score is on a different scale—such as the Delinquent scale.

3. Grouping adolescents according to the Internalizing-Externalizing dichotomy. This can be done by comparing those whose Internalizing score is well above their Externalizing score with those who show the opposite pattern. As discussed in Chapter 3, it is advisable to use a fairly stringent criterion for distinguishing between Internalizers and Externalizers, such as requiring that *(a)* their total problem score is in the clinical range, and *(b)* the dif-

ference between their Internalizing and Externalizing scores is at least 10 T score points. It should be remembered that, because Internalizing and Externalizing scores are positively correlated with each other, many adolescents are not clearly classifiable as Internalizers versus Externalizers. The more stringent the criterion used for separating them, the fewer will be classified, but the "purer" the groups will be.

4. Scores on the YSR problem scales can be compared with those on the YSR competence scales or other data—such as the CBCL or TRF—to distinguish between adolescents whose patterns are very similar across types of data and those whose patterns differ markedly across types of data. These groups can then be compared with respect to possible etiological differences.

Grouping by Etiology. A second way to use the YSR in etiological research is as a dependent variable for testing whether particular etiological differences are manifest in self-ratings. Suppose, for example, that we wish to determine whether a particular organic dysfunction is associated with particular self-reported problems. We could compare YSRs completed by adolescents who have the organic dysfunction with YSRs from otherwise similar adolescents who do not have the dysfunction.

If the YSR scores do not correlate with etiological differences confirmed in other ways, this may mean that either *(a)* the YSR is insensitive to differences between the self-perceptions of adolescents whose problems have different etiologies, or *(b)* the different etiologies do not produce differences in self-perceptions. To choose between these conclusions, it would be necessary to determine whether any other measure could detect differences in self-ratings that correlate with etiological differences. If we hypothesize that a particular organic dysfunction produces depression, but find that adolescents having this dysfunction are not deviant on the YSR Depressed scale, we should determine whether they are deviant on any other self-report measures of depression. If they are not, this would indicate that the hypothesized etiological factors do not result in high levels of self-reported depression.

Manipulation of Etiological Factors. A third approach to etiological research is to use the YSR as a dependent variable when etiological factors are manipulated. Suppose a drug, for example, is known to ameliorate an organic abnormality. By having adolescents afflicted with the abnormality fill out the YSR following administration of the drug versus a placebo, we can test the sensitivity of the YSR to changes in the organic abnormality. Conversely, if an unproven intervention is tried in hope of ameliorating abnormalities, the YSR can serve as a dependent variable for assessing change in response to the intervention. The specificity of a particular intervention's effect can also be assessed by determining whether adolescents differing in pre-intervention characteristics show different changes in their YSR responses following an intervention. Suppose we provide social skills training for adolescents who initially score high only on the Unpopular scale and those who score high on the Aggressive scale, as well as on the Unpopular scale. Do both groups show improvements on the YSR and other measures, or does the intervention have different effects on the two groups?

Outcome Studies

A basic question in the study of psychopathology is, "What typically happens to individuals having Disorder X?" If we knew what the outcome will be without intervention versus with Intervention A or Intervention B, we would be better able to decide which adolescents need professional help, what kind of help they need, and how to advise parents. We would also be able to concentrate research on disorders found to have poor outcomes, instead of those likely to be benign. The following sections illustrate some of the ways in which the YSR can be used in outcome research.

Longitudinal General Population Studies. One type of outcome research involves obtaining standardized assessment data on large general population samples and then reassessing them periodically to identify predictors of good and poor outcomes. If the YSR is used at the initial assessment and then at subsequent reassessments, it can be determined whether deviant scores on particular scales predict continued deviant scores in these areas. It can also be determined whether the YSR predicts pathological outcomes according to other measures such as parent reports, diagnostic interviews, referral for mental health services, suicidal behavior, and police contacts.

The applicability of the YSR to the adolescent period makes it especially useful for identifying precursors of early adult disorders. Because the YSR can be quickly and cheaply administered and scored, it is easy to use with large groups, such as all the pupils of a school system. An advantage of using large general population samples is that they can more adequately reflect the full range of variation in a population than can samples selected for having certain pre-existing characteristics. Capturing a broad range of variation is important for providing comprehensive tests of both the potential predictor variables and the outcome variables. However, the complexity of possible interrelations among variables can present formidable analytic challenges, and low prevalence rates may limit conclusions about particular disorders.

Groups at Risk. To obtain substantial numbers of subjects likely to develop a particular disorder, samples can be chosen from groups who are at statistically higher risk for the disorder than general population samples would be. The risk factors may be extrinsic to the adolescents, such as having a schizophrenic or alcoholic parent or living in a high delinquency area. Or the risk factors may involve characteristics of the adolescent, such as school failure, aggression, suicidal behavior, or referral for mental health services. By selecting a high risk sample, the number of eventual cases of a particular target disorder is expected to be larger than in a sample of similar size from the general population.

To trace the development of the target disorder in a high risk sample, initial standardized assessments should be made to obtain a baseline for the functioning of each subject and to obtain data on potential predictors of which subjects will develop disorders. Similar assessments can then be repeated at regular intervals to identify the individuals who actually do develop disorders, as well as to determine the timing and sequence in the development of disorders.

For studies of adolescents at risk, the YSR can be used as

one of the baseline assessment procedures and can then be repeated throughout adolescence. The YSR scores can be used to identify changes in self-reported problems and competencies, to compare each subject with the other subjects, and to compare the subjects with normative groups of agemates.

When it is found which individuals actually develop disorders, the previously assessed characteristics can be analyzed to identify those that were associated with good versus poor outcomes. Inferences can then be drawn about the specific causal factors that determine why some individuals at risk develop a particular disorder whereas others do not. The initial YSR scores may be found to predict good versus poor outcomes, and changes in YSR scores may be found to precede or accompany the emergence of the target disorders.

Outcome of Services. Adolescents who are referred for mental health or special educational services are of particular interest, because they are considered deviant enough to need professional help, and the service systems have opportunities to offer help. Although there have been follow-up studies of children and adolescents referred for mental health services (e. g., Robins, 1974), tests of the predictability of differential outcomes have been limited by the lack of standardization in the initial assessment data.

To enable outcome studies to tell us precisely what kind of cases have good outcomes and what kind have poor outcomes, all the cases must have the same initial data. Although outcomes may be affected by the treatment received and other variables beside the initial characteristics of the cases, too little is known about the typical outcomes for particular kinds of cases as they encounter typical services.

If the YSR is completed by adolescents referred to a service, follow-ups of the adolescents can be used to test whether those with particular YSR scores or profile patterns differ significantly in outcome. Other potential predictors should also be tested in such outcome studies, such as demographics, family constellation, and standardized ratings by informants, such as parents and teachers.

Outcome studies of services can be especially valuable for identifying the types of individuals who have poor outcomes. If characteristics assessed at intake are found to distinguish clearly between adolescents having poor versus good outcomes, this argues for finding new ways of helping adolescents like those found to have the poor outcomes. The possibilities for improvement include trying different interventions, referral to other types of services, and the development of new interventions. To test the effects of the interventions, experimental studies are usually needed, as discussed next.

Experimental Intervention Studies

To determine whether a particular intervention *causes* a better outcome than no intervention or a different intervention, it is usually necessary to experimentally manipulate the intervention conditions. Suppose, for example, that an outcome study showed that adolescents scoring high on the YSR Depressed and Aggressive scales had especially poor outcomes. Suppose that we therefore develop Intervention A designed for this group and wish to determine whether it yields better results than Intervention B or no intervention.

The YSR can be employed in several ways to test whether Intervention A is better than Intervention B or no intervention. First, because the adolescents to be tested are those with high scores on the YSR Depressed and Aggressive scales, the YSR is used to identify subjects for the study. Because all the subjects fill out the YSR prior to the intervention conditions, it provides a baseline measure against which to compare outcomes. After intervention, all the adolescents can be asked to fill out the YSR again. The postintervention scores can then be compared with preintervention scores for each intervention condition. Other measures, such as parent and teacher ratings, should also be used.

Beside being used to select subjects and to assess the effects of interventions, the YSR can be used to create matched groups to receive different intervention conditions. In a *randomized blocks design*, for example, subgroups of subjects (called "blocks") are first matched with respect to YSR scores and other important variables, such as age, sex, and SES. The members of a block are then randomly assigned to the different intervention conditions. If there are three intervention conditions, each member of a block of subjects is randomly assigned to a different one of the three conditions. If the interventions can be varied for the same individuals—such as an active drug alternated with a placebo—matched groups can be formed to receive the interventions in different orders. Some subjects thus receive the drug first followed by the placebo. Other subjects matched to them for YSR scores and other characteristics receive the opposite order.

Studies of Diagnostic Constructs

The YSR can be used in studies of particular diagnostic constructs. If we wish to study depression as a diagnostic construct, for example, high scores on the YSR Depressed scale can be used as one criterion for selecting depressed adolescents, while low scores on the Depressed scale are used for selecting a nondepressed comparison group. Other measures designed specifically to assess depression as a diagnostic construct could also be used. A multidimensional measure such as the YSR has the advantage of showing whether an adolescent reports problems only in the target area or in other areas as well. If we measure only one syndrome, we will not know whether an adolescent who is deviant in that syndrome is also deviant in other areas. To form groups who are relatively "pure" with respect to a particular diagnostic construct, it is important to insure that they are not too heterogeneous with respect to other types of problems.

The YSR as an Indicator of Other Problems

Beside the syndromes yielded by our factor analyses of the YSR, other groups of items may be consistently related to particular types of problems. If YSRs are completed by adolescents known to have a particular type of problem, they can be compared with YSRs completed by adolescents not having that problem to determine whether there are consistent differences. YSRs completed by sexually abused adolescents, for example, can be compared with those completed by demographically similar nonabused adolescents. Because abuse may be associated with a variety of behavioral/emotional problems, it would be advisable to compare abused adolescents with clinically-referred nonabused adolescents, as well as with normal adolescents. By including a clinical comparison group, we can determine whether there are particular items that distinguish abused adolescents from those distressed for other reasons. If particular items are found to distinguish adolescents who have a type of problem not directly assessed by the YSR, such as sex abuse, the YSR can then be used as an aid in identifying new cases having this type of problem.

SUMMARY

The YSR is designed to obtain standardized self-reports that will aid practitioners in making decisions about particular adolescents and researchers in addressing more general questions. Practical applications to helping individual adolescents include the following:

1. As part of the intake procedure in mental health services.

2. As a take-off point for interviewing adolescents.

3. As a component of multiaxial assessment encompassing parent data, teacher data, cognitive assessment, physical assessment, and other forms of direct assessment of the adolescent, including interviews and direct observations.

4. As a basis for planning interventions.

5. For reassessments during and after treatment.

6. As a basis for determining eligibility for special school services.

7. As an aid in making diagnoses.

We outlined the correspondence of the YSR, CBCL, TRF, and DOF to PL94-142 criteria for severe emotional disturbance, as well as to DSM-III-R diagnostic categories. We also discussed use of the YSR in relation to physical illness, handicaps, and forensic evaluations.

Beside practical applications to helping individual adolescents, the YSR is designed to address questions about groups of adolescents, such as the following:

1. *Needs assessments* to determine the number of adolescents in a particular population likely to need help for particular types of problems.

2. *Accountability for services*, including documentation of problems for which adolescents are referred, reporting of service activities, justifying requests for funding, program planning, and program evaluation.

Applications to more formal research endeavors include the following:

1. Epidemiological research.

2. Etiological research.

3. Outcome studies.

4. Experimental intervention studies.

5. Studies of diagnostic constructs.

6. Use of the YSR as an indirect indicator of other problems, such as abuse experienced by the adolescent.

Chapter 9
Answers to Commonly
Asked Questions

The purpose of this chapter is to answer questions that occasionally arise about the YSR and profile. Although earlier sections of the *Manual* address many of these questions, we list them here to provide explicit answers, supplemented by references to more detailed information where relevant. The questions are grouped according to whether they refer mainly to the content of the YSR, scoring the YSR, or the YSR profile. If you have a question that is not found under one heading, look under the other headings as well. The Table of Contents and Index may also help you find answers to questions not listed here.

QUESTIONS ABOUT THE YSR

1. Why is the YSR said to have 102 specific problem items and 16 socially desirable items, when the item numbers only go to 112?

Answer: Item *56* includes seven specific physical complaints designated as *a* through *g*. Combined with the remaining 95 specifically stated problems, this sums to 102 problem items. In addition, item *56h* provides space for respondents to enter any physical problems not otherwise listed. Total problem scores are computed as the sum of 1s and 2s for the 102 specific problem items + item *56h*. If a 2 is scored for all 102 items and *56h*, the total score would be 206.

2. What is done with the 16 socially desirable items?

Answer: These items were inserted to replace CBCL problem items that were deemed inappropriate to ask adolescents. To mitigate the list of problem items, they refer to socially desirable characteristics that most adolescents can endorse about themselves. Because most adolescents do, in fact, endorse them, they do not discriminate well between referred and nonreferred groups, and they are not scored on the YSR profile.

3. **Why doesn't the YSR have items for special class placement, grade repetition, and school problems like those on the CBCL?**

   Answer: These items were omitted from the YSR, because they were deemed to be potentially embarassing to adolescents and less accurately reported by adolescents than by their parents or teachers. Page 2 of the YSR does provide space for the adolescent to "describe any concerns or problems you have about school." The responses entered here are clinically useful, but they are not scored on the YSR profile.

4. **What if an adolescent's reading skills are poor?**

   Answer: If an adolescent's reading skills are below the 5th grade reading level, the YSR should be read aloud by an interviewer who records the adolescent's answers. If the adolescent's reading skills are questionable, one copy of the YSR can be handed to the adolescent while the interviewer retains a second copy. The interviewer then says: "I'm going to read the questions on this form and I'll write down your answers." Most adolescents who can read adequately will soon start answering the questions before they are read, but this procedure avoids embarrassment for those who cannot read well. If the YSR is administered orally, it should be done in a private location, out of earshot of others.

5. **What if an adolescent can't read English but can read another language?**

   Answer: At this writing, we know of translations of the CBCL into 23 languages. Contact Dr. Achenbach for the current status of YSR translations.

6. **Can the YSR be used for ages below 11 and over 18?**

   Answer: We did not norm the YSR below the age of 11, because too large a proportion of younger children—especially those referred for mental health services—would have inadequate cognitive or reading skills. We did not norm the

YSR above the age of 18, because many of the items are less relevant beyond that age and it is difficult to obtain representative general population samples during the period of transition between the family of origin and young adults' establishment of their own households. Although the YSR can be used with bright 9- and 10-year-olds and with some 19- and 20-year-olds, the user should be aware that the norms are not directly applicable to these ages. For respondents outside the target age range, the focus should therefore be on the specific content of responses, comparisons between the same respondents' raw scores on different occasions, and comparisons between respondents of the same age.

7. **Can the YSR be used with physically or mentally handicapped adolescents?**

   Answer: The norms for the YSR are based on representative general population samples of adolescents free of major handicaps. If handicapped adolescents are capable of responding to the YSR either by filling it out themselves or by responding orally, their responses are valuable for identifying specific areas of concern, for assessing change from one occasion to another, and for comparison with normative samples of nonhandicapped adolescents. This may be especially useful for evaluating handicapped adolescents who must mix with nonhandicapped people, as in mainstream situations. Even though a handicap is known to contribute to particular problems, it is still important to know the specific forms and degrees of deviance indicated by the adolescent's self-report. However, a mental age of at least 10 years is needed to ensure adequate comprehension of the items.

8. **Page 3 of the YSR instructs the respondent to base ratings on the previous 6 months. What if the user wants the respondent to focus on a shorter period or wants to readminister the YSR over intervals of less than 6 months?**

   Answer: The 6-month instruction can be changed to suit the interval desired. If the interval is reduced much below 6 months, this may reduce scores on some items and scales. Low frequency problems, such as suicide attempts and fire-setting, may also be missed if the rating interval is too short. If reassessments are planned for intervals of less than 6 months, however, the instructions should be changed to use the same shortened interval for each rating. If follow-up ratings are to be done after a 3-month interval, for example, the respondent should be instructed to base both the initial and follow-up ratings on 3-month periods. Otherwise, scores may be higher at one rating merely because a longer rating period was specified than for the other rating. Although brief intervals are not recommended for raters such as parents because time is required for them to become aware of changes in behavior, intervals as short as a few days or a week may be acceptable for self-ratings to monitor responses to specific interventions. It should be remembered, however, that the shorter the interval on which ratings are based, the more vulnerable the results are to random and transient changes.

9. **Is there a short form of the YSR that takes less time to fill out?**

    Answer: There is not a short form as such. However, the competence portion of the YSR (pages 1 and 2) or problem portion (pages 3 and 4) can be administered alone. Because each of these is brief and each scale's scores require that all the constituent items of the scale are considered by the respondent, it would not make sense to abbreviate the YSR any farther.

10. **Is there a machine-readable form of the YSR?**

    Answer: We have not developed machine-readable YSR forms, because *(a)* several items must be described by the respondent and then judged by a person familiar with the rules for scoring the YSR; *(b)* machine-readable forms are more susceptible to response errors that are hard to detect; *(c)* machine-readable forms make it hard to take account of the comments that adolescents often write on the YSR.

SCORING THE YSR

(Appendix A provides detailed scoring instructions, including criteria for items the respondent is asked to describe.)

1. **What if the respondent scores two items when his/her comments indicate that they both refer to exactly the same problem?**

   Answer: Score only the item that most specifically describes the problem. For example, suppose a respondent circled 2 for item *9. I can't get my mind off certain thoughts (describe)* and wrote in "sex." And the respondent also circled 2 for item *96. I think about sex too much.* Because item *96* covers the problem more specifically than item *9,* only the 2 for item *96* should be counted, whereas item *9* should be rescored as 0.

2. **What if a boy writes in "girls" for item *9. I can't get my mind off certain thoughts (describe)?***

   Answer: On the CBCL and TRF, item *9* includes the word *obsessions* and is scored to exclude problems that are clearly not obsessional. Because adolescents may not be familiar with the term "obsession," it is not included in the YSR item. Furthermore, adolescents' reports of preoccupying thoughts are apt to be important even if they do not qualify as obsessions. The scoring of item *9* is therefore not as restrictive on the YSR as on the CBCL and TRF. Except for responses that are more specifically covered by other items, as illustrated in #1 above, YSR item *9* should be scored as the adolescent respondent scored it. Thus, even though it might be quite normal for an adolescent boy to be preoccupied with girls, the score entered by the adolescent should be left intact. (Note that, if the respondent had written "sex" for item *9,* item *96* should be scored instead, as described in #1 above.)

3. **What if a respondent writes "ringing in ears" for item *40. I hear things that nobody else seems able to hear (describe)* or writes "spots before eyes" for item *70. I see things that nobody else seems able to see (describe)?***

Answer: As with item *9*, these items should be scored as the adolescent respondent scored them, unless the descriptions indicate that they are more specifically covered by another item. Although items *40* and *70* load on the Thought Disorder scale for both sexes, they also load on the Somatic Complaints scale for girls. Because adolescents who are unlikely to have reality-testing problems occasionally score these items for experiences such as ringing in ears and spots before eyes, it should not be assumed that these items are always indicative of poor reality testing.

4. **What if the respondent circles two scores for a particular item or otherwise indicates that the item is true but does not clearly indicate a score of 1 or 2?**

   Answer: Score the item 1.

5. **How is item *56h* figured in the total score?**

   Answer: If the respondent has entered for item *56h* a physical problem without known medical cause that is not specifically covered by an item listed on the YSR, add the 1 or 2 scored by the respondent for *56h* to the 1s and 2s for all other problem items. If the respondent has entered more than one additional physical problem, count only the one having the highest score. Thus, if a respondent gave one additional physical problem a score of 1 and another additional physical problem a score of 2, add 2 to the total problem score. (Adding a maximum of 2 points for item *56h* is intended to limit the amount of variance contributed by items that are not stated for other adolescents to rate.)

6. **What is done with responses to the open-ended item regarding school concerns on page 2 and "anything else that describes your feelings, behavior, or interests" on page 4?**

   Answer: The entries in these spaces are often clinically useful and helpful as a basis for interviewing adolescents, but they are not scored.

7. **Should YSRs that have many unanswered items be scored?**

   Answer: The scoring instructions (Appendix A) give rules for dealing with unanswered items. In brief, if one item is omitted from the Activities or Social scale, the mean of the other five items of that scale is substituted for the missing item. If more than one item is missing from either of these scales, do *not* score the scale. Do *not* score School Performance if the respondent checked boxes for *less than 3* academic subjects. Do *not* compute the total competence score unless scores are available for Activities, Social, and School Performance. On the problem portion of the YSR, do *not* compute scale scores or the total problem score if *more than 8* problem items were left blank (not counting item *56h*), unless it is clear that the respondent intended the blanks to be zeroes.

8. How is the total problem score used?

Answer: The sum of 1s and 2s for all the problem items (maximum score $= 206$) provides a global index of self-reported problems. We have found that scores at the 89th percentile of the normative samples (raw score $= 68$ for boys; 70 for girls) provide good cutoffs for marking the upper end of the normal range. Scores higher than these are considered to be in the clinical range. The total problem score can also be used as a global index for comparing self-reported problems between different groups and for assessing change as a function of time or interventions.

9. Why isn't there a cutoff on the total competence score?

Answer: As detailed in Chapter 5, the total competence score was not found to discriminate effectively betweeen clinically-referred and nonreferred adolescents. The competence score is a useful global index of self-reported positive characteristics and may be useful for assessing changes in self-reported competencies over time. However, the lack of a clear difference between the scores of our clinical and normative samples argues against establishing a clinical cutoff on the competence score.

THE YSR PROFILE

1. How can hand scoring be made quicker and easier?

Answer: We offer scoring templates that fit over the YSR to indicate the scales on which the problem items are scored. Scoring usually becomes quicker with experience. Certain scores can be omitted if you do not need them, such as the Internalizing and Externalizing scores. Some users may prefer to obtain only the total problem score or only the Internalizing and Externalizing scores, which can be done quickly. If we grouped the problem items on the YSR according to their profile scales, this might make scoring easier. However, it could create a halo effect on the respondent's ratings and would require different YSRs for each sex, because the problem items are not all scored on the same scales for both sexes. We recommend computer scoring whenever feasible. Contact Dr. Achenbach for information on computer-scoring programs.

2. Why are some problems included on more than one profile scale?

Answer: An item is included on every scale derived from a factor on which the item loaded $\geq.30$. Chapter 2 explains the rationale for retaining items on more than one scale if they loaded $\geq.30$ on more than one factor.

3. Doesn't the inclusion of some items on Internalizing and Externalizing scales create an artifactual correlation between these groupings?

Answer: As explained in Chapter 3, Internalizing and Externalizing problems are positively correlated with each other even when overlapping items are deleted. Like measures of ability, measures of problems tend to be positively correlated with each other—individuals who have many problems of one type tend to be at least above average on other types, too. Chapter 3 details procedures for categorizing adolescents according to whether they primarily report Internalizing or Externalizing problems.

4. Why are there no norms for the "Other Problems" listed on the profile?

Answer: The "Other Problems" on the profile do not constitute a scale, but are merely problems that did not load $\geq .30$ on any of the factors retained for that sex. There are thus no associations among them to warrant treating them as a scale. However, they are included in the total problem score.

5. Should extremely low scores on any problem scales be considered deviant?

Answer: Low scores merely reflect the absence of reported problems. As explained in Chapter 2, the profile compresses the low end of the narrow-band problem scales, so that 55 is the minimum T score obtainable on these scales. If a user wishes to retain all the differentiation possible at the low end of these scales, raw scores can be employed. However, it should be remembered that all the scores below a T score of 55 are well within the normal range. They should not, therefore, be construed as indicating different degrees of deviance. Extremely low total problem scores may suggest that the respondent has not understood the YSR or has not been candid, as discussed in answer to Question 9.

6. Should there be separate norms for different socioeconomic or racial groups?

Answer: Chapter 5 shows that socioeconomic and racial differences are generally too small to warrant separate norms.

7. How can comparisons be made between profile scores for boys and girls?

Answer: Because there are sex differences in the patterning and prevalence of problems, we derived problem scales separately from YSRs completed by boys and girls. We also normed all competence and problem scales separately for each sex. Although six of the syndromes found were similar enough for boys and girls to warrant the same names, the exact composition of the syndromes and the distributions of scores differ between the sexes. However, if a user wishes to include YSR scores for boys and girls in the same analyses, we suggest using T scores appropriate for the sex of each respondent on all the scales that are comparable for the two sexes. The comparable scales are: Activities, Social, total competence, all the narrow-band problem scales except Self-Destructive/Identity Problems (which exists only for boys), Internalizing, Externalizing, and total problem score. When data from both sexes are combined in the same analysis, however, it is always advisable to retain sex as a dimension of the analysis, both to take account of sex differences in the distribution of scores and to identify any interactions between sex and other variables.

8. How are interpretations of the profile made?

Answer: The YSR profile is intended as a standardized summary of the competencies and problems reported by an adolescent and compared to those reported by other adolescents of the same sex. As such, it is to be compared and integrated with everything else that is known about the adolescent, instead of being "interpreted" in isolation. Additional relevant data include other people's descriptions of the adolescent—such as parents' reports on the CBCL, teachers' reports on the TRF, and observers' reports on the DOF; developmental history; tests of cognitive ability, academic achievement, and perceptual-motor functioning; biomedical data; and clinical interviews and observations. Guidelines are provided in Chapter 8, while a variety of case illustrations are presented in a book by Achenbach and McConaughy (1987).

9. Is there a "lie" scale for the profile?

Answer: Deliberate lying is only one type of bias that can lead to excessively low or high scores, depending on whether the respondent denies or exaggerates problems. Social desirability sets, overscrupulousness, and misunderstandings can also affect ratings. In view of the variety of possible biases, we did not add items intended to detect every possible type of bias. Instead, we stress that profile scores should never be used to make decisions in isolation from other information about the respondent. The scores should always be compared with other data to identify major discrepancies or distortions and to determine the reasons. Extremely low or high scores for competence or problems should always be followed up to determine whether they accurately reflect the respondents' views of themselves. If they accurately reflect the respondents' views, do these views differ markedly from the views of others, such as parents, teachers, and clinicians?

Because most adolescents report a substantial number of problems, extremely low scores are so uncommon as to suggest that the respondent has not understood the YSR or is not being candid. Total problem scores below 5 for boys and below 6 for girls were obtained by less than 2% of the adolescents in our normative samples and should therefore be followed up to determine whether they accurately reflect the respondents' views. Scores from 6 to 10 for boys and 7 to 14 for girls are low enough to hint at a tendency to deny problems, but might accurately reflect the respondents' views.

Based on the distributions of total problem scores in our clinical samples, scores above 168 for boys and 151 for girls are so *high* as to raise questions about exaggeration or misunderstanding.

10. **Why aren't there any YSR "profile types" like those for the parent version of the Child Behavior Profile?**

Answer: We performed cluster analyses of YSR profiles for large samples of referred adolescents, using procedures like those described in Chapter 8 of the *Manual* for the CBCL (Achenbach & Edelbrock, 1983). We did not find as clear differentiation among YSR profile types as among CBCL profile types, however. We will continue experimenting with the classification of YSR profile patterns, but it does not currently appear that they provide as good a basis for a typology as the CBCL profiles do.

11. **Why is there no School scale on the YSR profile?**

Answer: As discussed in Chapters 1 and 2, we did not deem it appropriate to have adolescents report special class placement, repeating grades, and school problems as parents report them on the CBCL. Because the only school item scorable on the competence portion of the YSR is the adolescent's self-ratings for performance in academic subjects, this is an insufficient basis for a separate scale. How ever, the mean of the adolescent's self-ratings for academic performance is included in the total competence score.

REFERENCES

Abramowitz, M., & Stegun, I. A. (1968). *Handbook of mathematical functions*. Washington, D.C.: National Bureau of Standards.

Achenbach, T. M. (1966). The classification of children's psychiatric symptoms: A factor-analytic study. *Psychological Monographs, 80*, (Whole No. 615).

Achenbach, T. M. (1985). *Assessment and taxonomy of child and adolescent psychopathology*. Beverly Hills, CA: Sage.

Achenbach, T. M., & Edelbrock, C. (1978). The classification of child psychopathology: A review and analysis of empirical efforts. *Psychological Bulletin, 85*, 1275-1301.

Achenbach, T. M., & Edelbrock, C. (1981). Behavioral problems and competencies reported by parents of normal and disturbed children aged four to sixteen. *Monographs of the Society for Research in Child Development, 46*, Serial No. 188.

Achenbach, T. M., & Edelbrock, C. (1983). *Manual for the Child Behavior Checklist and Revised Child Behavior Profile*. Burlington, VT: University of Vermont Department of Psychiatry.

Achenbach, T. M., & Edelbrock, C. (1986). *Manual for the Teacher's Report Form and Teacher Version of the Child Behavior Profile*. Burlington, VT: University of Vermont Department of Psychiatry.

Achenbach, T. M., & McConaughy, S. H. (1987). *Empirically-based assessment of child and adolescent psychopathology: Practical applications*. Beverly Hills, CA: Sage.

Achenbach, T. M., McConaughy, S. H., & Howell, C. T. (1987). Child/adolescent behavioral and emotional problems: Implications of cross-informant correlations for situational specificity. *Psychological Bulletin, 101*, 213-232.

Achenbach, T. M., Verhulst, F. C., Baron, G. D., & Akkerhuis, G. W. (1987). Epidemiological comparisons of Dutch and American children: I. Behavioral/emotional problems and competencies reported by parents for ages 4 to 16. *Journal of the American Academy of Child and*

Adolescent Psychiatry, *26*, 317-325.

Achenbach, T. M., Verhulst, F. C., Baron, G. D., & Althaus, M. (1987). A comparison of syndromes derived from the Child Behavior Checklist for American and Dutch boys aged 6-11 and 12-16. *Journal of Child Psychology and Psychiatry*, *28*, 437-453.

Achenbach, T. M., Verhulst, F. C., Edelbrock, C., Baron, G. D., & Akkerhuis, G. W. (1987). Epidemiologic comparisons of American and Dutch children: II. Behavioral/emotional problems reported by teachers for ages 6 to 11. *Journal of the American Academy of Child and Adolescent Psychiatry*, *26*, 326-332.

American Psychiatric Association. (3rd ed. 1980; 3rd ed. rev. 1987). *Diagnostic and statistical manual of mental disorders*. Washington, D.C.: Author.

Cohen, J. (1977). *Statistical power analysis for the behavioral sciences* (rev. ed.). New York: Academic Press.

Edelbrock, C. (1984, October). Relations between the NIMH Diagnostic Interview Schedule for Children (DISC) and the Child Behavior Checklist and Profile. Presented at the American Academy of Child Psychiatry, Toronto.

Edelbrock, C., Costello, A. J., & Kessler, M. D. (1984). Empirical corroboration of attention deficit disorder. *Journal of the American Academy of Child Psychiatry*, *23*, 285-290.

Edelbrock, C., Costello, A. J., Dulcan, M. K., Kalas, R., & Conover, N. C. (1985). Age differences in the reliability of the psychiatric interview of the child. *Child Development*, *56*, 265-275.

Evans, W. R. (1975). The Behavior Problem Checklist. Data from an inner city population. *Psychology in the Schools*, *12*, 301-303.

Feild, H. S., & Armenakis, A. A. (1974). On use of multiple tests of significance in psychological research. *Psychological Reports*, *35*, 427-431.

Gorsuch, R. L. (1983). *Factor analysis* (2nd ed.). Hillsdale, NJ: Erlbaum.

Harter, S. (1982). The Perceived Competence Scale for Children. *Child Development*, *53*, 87-97.

Hollingshead, A. B. (1975). *Four factor index of social status.* Unpublished paper. New Haven, CT: Yale University Department of Sociology.

Kazdin, A. E., French, N. H., & Unis, A. S. (1983). Child, mother, and father evaluations of depression in psychiatric inpatient children. *Journal of Abnormal Child Psychology, 11,* 167-180.

Milich, R., Roberts, M., Loney, J., & Caputo, J. (1980). Differentiating practice effects and statistical regression on the Conners Hyperkinesis Index. *Journal of Abnormal Child Psychology, 8,* 549-552.

Miller, L. C. (1967). Louisville Behavior Checklist for males, 6-12 years of age. *Psychological Reports, 21,* 885-896.

Miller, L. C., Hampe, E., Barrett, C. L., & Noble, H. (1972). Test-retest reliability of parent ratings of children's deviant behavior. *Psychological Reports, 31,* 249-250.

Peterson, D. R. (1961). Behavior problems of middle childhood. *Journal of Consulting Psychology, 25,* 205-209.

Piers, E. V. (1972). Parent predictions of children's self-concepts. *Journal of Consulting and Clinical Psychology, 38,* 428-433.

Quay, H. C. (1986). Classification. In H. C. Quay & J. S. Werry (Eds.), *Psychopathological disorders of childhood* (3rd ed.). New York: Wiley.

Robins, L. N. (1974). *Deviant children grown up* (2nd ed.). Huntington, NY: Krieger.

Robins, L. N. (1985). Epidemiology: Reflections on testing the validity of psychiatric interviews. *Archives of General Psychiatry, 42,* 918-924.

Sakoda, J. M., Cohen, B. H., & Beall, G. (1954). Test of significance for a series of statistical tests. *Psychological Bulletin, 51,* 172-175.

Zimet, S. G., & Farley, G. K. (1986). Four perspectives on the competence and self-esteem of emotionally disturbed children beginning day treatment. *Journal of the American Academy of Child Psychiatry, 25,* 76-83.

Zimet, S. G., & Farley, G. K. (1987). How do emotionally disturbed children report their competencies and self-worth? *Journal of the American Academy of Child and Adolescent Psychiatry, 26,* 33-38.

APPENDIX A
Instructions for Hand-Scoring
the Youth Self-Report Profile

Scoring the Competence Scales

Note. There are some small differences between the hand-scored and computer-scored data entry formats, but they produce the same results. Templates are available to assist in transferring data from pp. 3-4 of the YSR to the Profile. Be sure to use templates and the side of the profile appropriate for the sex of the respondent.

ACTIVITIES SCALE—Do **not** score if data are missing for more than 1 of the 6 scores indicated beside the Roman numerals below. The Roman numerals correspond to those on pages 1 and 2 of the YSR and on the profile scoring form. If a youth checks more than 1 box where only 1 should be checked, score the average of the 2 boxes checked.

I-A. # of sports. If youth reports 0 or 1 sport—enter 0 on profile
2 sports—enter 1
3 or more sports—enter 2

I-B. Mean of participation & skill in sports. If youth reports no sports, enter 0.
For each response of "less than average" or "below average"—score 0
"average"—score 1
"more than average" or "above average"—score 2

Excluding blanks and "don't know" responses, compute the **mean** of these scores by summing them and dividing by the number of scores you have summed. Enter this mean on the profile.

II-A. # of other activities. If youth reports 0 or 1 activity—enter 0 on profile
2 activities—enter 1
3 or more activities—enter 2
Do not count listening to radio or TV, goofing off, or the like as activities.

II-B. Mean of participation & skill in activities. Compute in the same way as specified in I-B for sports.

IV-A. # of jobs. If youth reports 0 or 1 job—enter 0 on profile
2 jobs—enter 1
3 or more jobs—enter 2

IV-B. Mean job quality. Compute as specified in I-B.

Total score for Activities Scale. Sum the 6 scores just entered. If missing data prevent computation of 1 score, substitute the **mean** of the other 5 for the missing score in computing the total. Round off total to nearest .5.

SOCIAL SCALE—Do **not** score if data are missing for more than 1 of the 6 scores.

III-A. # of organizations. If youth reports 0 or 1—enter 0 on profile
                                                    2—enter 1
                                        3 or more—enter 2

III-B. Mean of participation in organizations. Compute as specified in I-B.

V-1. # of friends. If youth reports 0 or 1—enter 0 on profile
                                          2 or 3—enter 1
                                      4 or more—enter 2

V-2. Contacts with friends. If youth reports "less than 1"—enter 0 on profile
(If youth checked "None" in V-1, enter 0)   "1 or 2"—enter 1
                                              "3 or more"—enter 2

VI-A. Behavior with others. For each of the first three items (items a, b, & c),
                        if the youth checks "worse"—score 0
                              "about the same"—score 1
                                      "better"—score 2

Excluding any items for which the youth did not check a box, compute the **mean** of these scores and enter it on the profile.

VI-B. Do things by self. (Item d)
                        If the youth checks "worse"—enter 0 on profile
                              "about the same"—enter 1
                                      "better"—enter 2

Total score for Social Scale. Sum the 6 scores just entered. If missing data prevent computation of 1 score, substitute the **mean** of the other 5 for the missing score in computing the total. Round off total to nearest .5.

SCHOOL PERFORMANCE—This does not constitute a profile scale, but it is added to scores for Activities and Social to obtain a total competence score. Do **not** score if youth has checked boxes for **less than 3** academic subjects.

VII. Mean performance. For each academic subject checked "failing"—score 0
                              "below average"—score 1
                                    "average"—score 2
                              "above average"—score 3

Compute the **mean** of these scores, rounded to the nearest .5. (Academic subjects include reading, writing, math, spelling, science, computer courses, English, foreign language, history, social studies; do **not** count physical education, art, music, home economics, driver education, industrial arts, typing, or the like.)

Note. Comments written by youth in the space below item VII are **not** scored on the profile.

Optional. A total competence score can be obtained by summing the total raw scores for Activities, Social, and School. Do **not** compute a total competence score unless scores are available for all 3 of these. *T* scores for total competence scores are at the end of these instructions.

Scoring the Problem Scales

Do **not** score if data are missing for more than 8 items, not counting #56h. If a youth circles two numbers for an item, score the item 1. Note that there are 103 problem items, even though the numbers range from 1-112. Items 56a-h comprise 8 items and the following 16 items are socially desirable items that are excluded from the problem scores: 6, 15, 28, 49, 59, 60, 73, 78, 80, 88, 92, 98, 106, 107, 108, 109. Comments written by youth at the bottom of page 4 are **not** scored on the profile.

1. Item scores. If the youth circled 1 or 2 beside an item, enter the 1 or 2 on the appropriate scale of the profile. Note that some items are scored on more than one scale. Items that do not belong to any scale are listed under the heading 'Other Problems" on the Profile. Comments written by the youth should be used in judging whether items deserve to be scored, with the following guidelines:

a. For each problem reported by the youth, score only the YSR item that most specifically describes the problem. If the youth's comments show that more than one item has been scored for a particular problem, or if the youth writes in a problem for #56h that is specifically covered elsewhere, count only the most specific item.

b. For extreme behaviors (e.g., sets fires, attempts suicide)—if youth notes that it happened once but circles 0 or leaves it blank, score 1 unless it clearly happened earlier than the interval specified in the rating instructions (e.g., 6 months).

c. For items on which youth notes "used to do this," score as the youth scored it, unless it clearly occurred earlier than the interval specified in the instructions.

d. When in doubt, score item the way the youth scored it, with these exceptions:

item 9, can't get mind off certain thoughts—this item is not restricted to obsessions and can include almost anything the youth lists here except problems that are specifically listed elsewhere. If the youth wrote "sex" for this item, for example, it would be more appropriately scored under item 96, I think about sex too much. If not covered by another item, responses that might be considered normal for the youth's age should be scored the way the youth scored them; e.g., "cars," "girls," "boys."

item 40, hears things, & 70, sees things—score experiences such as "ringing in ears" and "spots before eyes" the way the youth scored them; do not score experiences while under the influence of drugs or alcohol.

item 46, nervous movements—if "can't sit still" or anything entirely covered by item 10 is entered here, score only item 10.

item 56d, problems with eyes—do not score "wear glasses," "near-sighted," and other visual problems having an organic basis.

item 66, repeats actions—this item is not restricted to compulsions and can include almost anything the youth lists here except problems that are specifically listed elsewhere. Speech repetitions or stammers, for example, would be more appropriately scored under item 79, speech problem.

item 77, sleeps more than most—do not score "want to stay in bed," but score difficulties in waking up.

item 84, strange behavior & 85, strange ideas—if what the youth describes is specifically covered by another item, score the more specific item instead.

item 105, alcohol or drugs—do not score tobacco or medication.

2. Scale scores. To obtain the total raw score for each problem scale, sum the 1s and 2s you have entered for each scale. Because the items listed under "Other Problems" do not form a scale, a total score is not computed for them.

Optional: # of problem items and total problem score. To compute the **number of items** scored as present, count the number of problem items scored 1 or 2. To compute the **total problem score**, sum the 1s and 2s for all problem items. These figures can be cross-checked by subtracting the number of items from the sum of 1s and 2s. The difference should equal the number of 2s. (The number and sum of items can **not** be computed by adding scale totals, because some items appear on more than one scale.) Be sure to **omit** the 16 nonproblem items from all computations of problem scores.

Graphic Display and *T* Scores

. To complete the graphic display for the competence and problem scales, make an X on the number above each scale that equals the total score obtained for that scale. The competence scale totals should be rounded to the nearest .5. When X's have been entered for all scales, connect the X's with a pencil.

Percentiles based on normative samples can be read from the left side of the graphic display. *T* scores can be read from the right side.

. *T* scores for Internalizing and Externalizing are listed in the box to the right of the problems profile. Enter the score (0, 1, or 2) for each problem item next to the item's number under the heading "Item." Sum the scores to get the Total Internalizing score and likewise for the Total Externalizing score. Under the heading "Total," find the total you have obtained. The score to the right of that number is the *T* score.

. *T* scores for total competence score and total problem score (sum of 1s and 2s) are listed on the following pages.

TOTAL COMPETENCE SCORES

T SCORE	BOYS RAW SCORES	GIRLS RAW SCORES	T SCORE	BOYS RAW SCORES	GIRLS RAW SCORES
10	0	0	46	-	14.0
11	.5	.5	47	15.0	14.5
12	1.0	-	48	15.5	15.0
13	1.5	1.0	49	16.0	15.5
14	2.0	1.5	50	-	-
15	2.5	2.0	51	16.5	16.0
16	3.0	2.5	52	17.0	16.5
17	3.5	-	53	-	17.0
18	4.0	3.0	54	17.5	-
19	4.5	3.5	55	18.0	17.5
20	-	4.0	56	-	18.0
21	5.0	4.5	57	18.5	18.5
22	5.5	-	58	19.0	-
23	6.0	5.0	59	-	19.0
24	6.5	5.5	60	19.5	-
25	7.0	6.0	61	20.0	19.5
26	7.5	6.5	62	20.5	20.0
27	8.0	-	63	-	20.5
28	8.5	7.0	64	21.0	-
29	9.0	7.5	65	-	21.0
30	-	-	66	-	-
31	9.5	8-8.5	67	21.5	-
32	10.0	9.0	68	-	21.5
33	10.5	9.5	69	22.0	-
34	11.0	10.0	70	-	22.0
35	-	-	71	-	22.5
36	11.5	10.5	72	22.5	-
37	-	11.0	73	-	-
38	12.0	-	74	23.0	23.0
39	-	11.5	75	23.5	23.5
40	12.5	12.0	76	24.0-24.5	24.0
41	13.0	-	77	25.0-25.5	24.5
42	-	12.5	78	26.0	25.0
43	13.5	13.0	79	-	-
44	14.0	-	80	26.5-27.0	25.5-27.0
45	14.5	13.5			

TOTAL PROBLEM SCORES

T SCORE	BOYS RAW SCORES	GIRLS RAW SCORES	T SCORE	BOYS RAW SCORES	GIRLS RAW SCORES
22	0	0-1	62	68^a-69	69-71(70^a)
23	1	2	63	70-72	72-74
24	2	3	64	73-74	75-76
25	3	4	65	75	77-78
26	4	5	66	76	79-81
27	5	-	67	77-79	82-83
29	-	6	68	-	84-85
30	-	7-8	69	80-84	86-88
31	6	9	70	85	89-90
32	7-8	10-11	71	86-90	91-93
33	9	12-13	72	91-95	94-97
34	10	14	73	96-99	98-100
35	-	15	74	100-103	101-103
36	11-13	16	75	104-108	104-106
37	14-15	17-19	76	109-112	107-110
38	16-17	20	77	113-117	111-113
39	-	21-22	78	118-121	114-116
40	18-19	23	79	122-126	117-120
41	20-22	24-25	80	127-130	121-123
42	23	26	81	131-134	124-126
43	24	27-28	82	135-139	127-129
44	25-26	29-30	83	140-143	130-133
45	27-28	31	84	144-148	134-136
46	29	32-33	85	149-152	137-139
47	30-31	34-35	86	153-156	140-142
48	32-33	36-37	87	157-161	143-146
49	34-35	38-39	88	162-165	147-149
50	36	40	89	166-169	150-153
51	37-39	41-42	90	170-173	154-158
52	40-41	43-44	91	174-176	159-163
53	42-43	45-46	92	177-180	164-168
54	44-45	47-48	93	181-183	169-173
55	46-48	49-51	94	184-187	174-178
56	49-50	52-53	95	188-190	179-183
57	51-53	54-55	96	191-193	184-188
58	54-56	56-58	97	194-197	189-193
59	57-60	59-62	98	198-200	194-198
60	61-63	63-64	99	201-204	199-203
61	64-67	65-68	100	205-206	204-206

[a]Upper limit of "normal" range for problem scores. There are no cutoffs for total competence scores.

APPENDIX B
Factor Loadings of Items on Problem Scales[a]

Boys Aged 11-18: 8-factor Varimax Rotation

Internalizing Scales

I. Depressed

103.	Sad	.54
112.	Worries	.53
71.	Self-conscious	.50
12.	Lonely	.49
13.	Confused	.47
54.	Overtired	.47
75.	Shy	.47
87.	Moody	.47
45.	Nervous	.46
69.	Secretive	.46
17.	Daydreams	.45
42.	Likes to be alone	.40
89.	Suspicious	.37
35.	Feels worthless	.35
46.	Twitches	.35
30.	Fears school	.33
31.	Fears impulses	.31
86.	Stubborn	.31
102.	Lacks energy	.31
9.	Can't get mind off certain thoughts	.30
	Eigenvalue	5.72

II. Unpopular

48.	Unliked	.61
38.	Is teased	.56
35.	Feels worthless	.52
34.	Feels persecuted	.46
25.	Doesn't get along with other kids	.44
33.	Feels unloved	.44
11.	Dependent	.40

II. Unpopular (cont'd)

43.	Lies, cheats	.40
19.	Seeks attention	.39
32.	Needs to be perfect	.39
1.	Acts young	.38
41.	Impulsive	.37
14.	Cries	.35
31.	Fears impulses	.35
50.	Anxious	.34
62.	Clumsy	.34
12.	Lonely	.33
45.	Nervous	.33
27.	Jealous	.32
30.	Fears school	.32
52.	Feels guilty	.31
13.	Confused	.31
20.	Destroys own things	.31
	Eigenvalue	5.67

Mixed Scales

III. Somatic Complaints

56c.	Nausea	.66
56f.	Stomachaches	.65
56b.	Headaches	.63
56a.	Pains	.61
56g.	Vomiting	.51
51.	Dizzy	.42
58.	Picking	.42
36.	Accident prone	.36
65.	Won't talk	.36
46.	Twitches	.32
54.	Overtired	.31
53.	Overeats	.30
	Eigenvalue	5.12

[a] Items are designated with the numbers they bear on the YSR and summaries of their content. For actual wording of items, see the YSR.

APPENDIX B (CONT'D)

IV. Self Destructive/
Identity Problems

18.	Harms self	.65
91.	Suicidal thoughts	.63
110.	Wishes to be opposite sex	.60
33.	Feels unloved	.45
35.	Feels worthless	.38
5.	Acts like opposite sex	.37
79.	Speech problems	.36
27.	Jealous	.30
103.	Sad	.30
	Eigenvalue	3.49

V. Thought Disorder

40.	Hears things	.69
70.	Sees things	.64
84.	Strange behavior	.58
85.	Strange thoughts	.49
79.	Speech problem	.41
66.	Repeats acts	.39
56g.	Vomiting	.35
83.	Stores up things	.34
9.	Can't get mind off certain thoughts	.33
47.	Nightmares	.33
29.	Fears	.30
56d.	Eye problems	.30
	Eigenvalue	3.70

Externalizing Scales

VI. Delinquent

82.	Steals outside home	.60
23.	Disobeys at school	.58
22.	Disobeys parents	.56
81.	Steals at home	.52
101.	Truant	.49

VI. Delinquent (cont'd)

21.	Destroys others' things	.48
97.	Threatens	.45
57.	Attacks people	.43
72.	Sets fires	.43
39.	Bad friends	.42
105.	Alcohol, drug	.42
43.	Lies, cheats	.41
67.	Runs away	.40
90.	Swears	.40
20.	Destroys own things	.39
41.	Impulsive	.37
86.	Stubborn	.37
63.	Prefers older kids	.36
37.	Fights	.34
61.	Poor schoolwork	.34
16.	Mean to others	.32
26.	Lacks guilt	.30
	Eigenvalue	5.37

VII. Aggressive

94.	Teases	.60
7.	Brags	.58
93.	Talks too much	.58
74.	Shows off	.54
95.	Temper	.52
104.	Loud	.52
3.	Argues	.51
97.	Threatens	.51
96.	Sex preocc.	.46
15.	Mean to others	.44
19.	Seeks attention	.41
90.	Swears	.41
68.	Screams	.38
89.	Suspicious	.37
39.	Bad friends	.31
86.	Stubborn	.31
57.	Attacks people	.30
	Eigenvalue	5.39

APPENDIX B (CONT'D)

Girls Aged 11-18: 8-factor Varimax Rotation

Internalizing Scales

I. Somatic Complaints

56a.	Pains	.67
56b.	Headaches	.63
56f.	Stomachaches	.61
56c.	Nausea	.59
56d.	Eye problems	.56
56g.	Vomiting	.47
51.	Dizzy	.46
29.	Fears	.39
46.	Twitches	.39
70.	Sees things	.38
40.	Hears things	.35
99.	Too neat	.34
76.	Little sleep	.32
47.	Nightmares	.31
56e.	Rashes	.30
	Eigenvalue	4.76

II. Depressed

103.	Sad	.72
35.	Feels worthless	.70
12.	Lonely	.68
112.	Worries	.63
13.	Confused	.61
45.	Nervous	.60
33.	Feels unloved	.59
71.	Self-conscious	.58
91.	Suicidal thoughts	.58
18.	Harms self	.57
14.	Cries	.55
75.	Shy	.52
50.	Anxious	.51
27.	Jealous	.50
52.	Feels guilty	.49
32.	Needs to be perfect	.48
54.	Overtired	.47
34.	Feels persecuted	.45

II. Depressed (cont'd)

31.	Fears impulses	.44
102.	Lacks energy	.43
62.	Clumsy	.42
17.	Daydreams	.41
8.	Trouble concentrating	.40
30.	Fears school	.40
87.	Moody	.39
48.	Unliked	.38
100.	Can't sleep	.38
24.	Doesn't eat well	.37
46.	Twitches	.33
51.	Dizzy	.33
89.	Suspicious	.32
9.	Can't get mind off certain thoughts	.31
	Eigenvalue	9.76

Mixed Scales

III. Unpopular

38.	Is teased	.57
48.	Unliked	.52
25.	Doesn't get along with kids	.51
1.	Acts young	.50
16.	Mean to others	.41
53.	Overeats	.40
111.	Avoids involvement	.33
64.	Prefers young kids	.32
11.	Dependent	.31
31.	Fears impulses	.31
37.	Fights	.31
	Eigenvalue	3.59

IV. Thought Disorder

84.	Strange behavior	.56
85.	Strange thoughts	.50
66.	Repeats acts	.49

APPENDIX B (CONT'D)

IV. Thought Disorder (cont'd)

40.	Hears things	.42
9.	Can't get mind off certain thoughts	.38
10.	Trouble sitting still	.38
83.	Stores up things	.35
8.	Trouble concentrating	.32
70.	Sees things	.32
69.	Secretive	.31
17.	Daydreams	.30
61.	Poor schoolwork	.30
	Eigenvalue	3.34

Externalizing Scales

V. Aggressive

95.	Temper	.57
97.	Threatens	.55
37.	Fights	.46
16.	Mean to others	.46
57.	Attacks people	.43
86.	Stubborn	.43
68.	Screams	.42
90.	Swears	.42
87.	Moody	.38
104.	Loud	.38
94.	Teases	.37
63.	Prefers older kids	.36
96.	Sex preoccupation	.34
89.	Suspicious	.32
34.	Feels persecuted	.32
3.	Argues	.31
69.	Secretive	.31
	Eigenvalue	4.30

VI. Delinquent

23.	Disobeys at school	.63
39.	Bad friends	.56
22.	Disobeys parents	.55
61.	Poor schoolwork	.49
82.	Steals outside home	.49
101.	Truant	.48
21.	Destroys others' things	.47
20.	Destroys own things	.46
90.	Swears	.46
43.	Lies, cheats	.44
81.	Steals at home	.44
105.	Alcohol, drug	.44
41.	Impulsive	.42
67.	Runs away	.42
8.	Trouble concentrating	.35
57.	Attacks people	.35
72.	Sets fires	.35
37.	Fights	.34
97.	Threatens	.33
	Eigenvalue	5.60

APPENDIX C

Mean Scale Scores for Boys

	Lower SES[a]		Middle SES[a]		Upper SES[a]		All SES Combined									
	T Score		T Score		T Score		T Score		SD of T		Raw Score		SD of Raw		SE of Mean	
	Ref.	Non.	Ref.	Non.	Ref.	Non.	Ref.	Non.	Ref.	Non.	Ref.	Non.	Ref.	Non.	Ref.	Non.
N =	116	121	147	139	103	128	366	388	366	388	366	388	366	388	366	388
Activities	49.9	47.8	48.8	48.8	50.3	50.7	49.6	49.1	6.7	6.9	7.4	7.1	2.2	2.1	.1	.1
Social	46.4	47.9	39.1	49.4	45.5	51.3	43.2	49.5	12.8	6.9	6.2	7.3	2.1	1.9	.1	.1
School[b]	2.0	2.1	1.8	2.3	2.1	2.4	—	—	—	—	2.0	2.3	.6	.6	.0	.0
Total Competence	50.7	48.9	46.5	50.9	50.5	55.6	49.1	51.9	10.5	10.1	15.8	16.8	3.5	3.4	.2	.2
Aggressive	59.9	58.4	59.2	57.0	59.8	56.2	60.0	57.2	7.5	4.4	11.7	9.3	6.4	5.3	.3	.3
Delinquent	60.4	58.4	60.1	56.8	60.3	56.1	60.2	57.1	7.2	4.1	12.1	8.1	7.2	5.5	.4	.3
Depressed	60.0	56.7	60.6	57.4	60.9	56.6	60.5	56.9	7.8	4.1	13.4	9.3	7.5	5.8	.4	.3
Self Destructive/ Identity Probs.	59.9	57.4	60.4	57.5	60.5	57.1	60.3	57.4	7.4	4.3	2.6	1.5	2.8	1.7	.1	.1
Somatic	60.0	57.9	59.6	57.2	60.4	56.3	59.9	57.1	7.7	4.6	5.5	3.7	4.4	3.2	.2	.2
Thought Disorder	63.2	58.0	61.1	57.4	61.1	56.6	61.8	57.3	7.9	4.4	5.3	3.0	3.9	2.5	.2	.1
Unpopular	60.2	56.9	59.8	57.1	60.8	56.4	60.2	56.8	7.3	3.7	11.9	7.6	7.7	5.5	.4	.3
Internalizing	56.2	50.4	56.4	50.2	57.6	49.7	56.7	50.1	11.0	9.3	22.3	15.2	12.2	9.2	.6	.5
Externalizing	56.0	53.1	55.9	50.2	56.2	48.9	56.0	50.7	10.7	9.3	19.9	14.6	10.6	8.4	.6	.4
Total Problems	56.9	51.5	56.3	50.1	57.5	48.4	56.8	50.0	10.9	9.4	55.5	39.0	26.7	19.6	1.4	1.0

[a] Hollingshead (1975) occupational levels 1-3.5 = lower SES; 4-6.5 = middle SES; 7-9 = upper SES.
[b] Raw scores only, because no T scores are computed for the School score.

APPENDIX C (CONT'D)

Mean Scale Scores for Girls

	Lower SES[a]		Middle SES[a]		Upper SES[a]		All SES Combined							
	T Score		T Score		T Score		T Score		SD of T		Raw Score		SD of Raw		SE of Mean
	Ref.	Non.	Ref.	Non.	Ref.	Non.	Ref.	Non.	Ref.	Non.	Ref.	Non.	Ref.	Non.	Ref.	Non.
N =	102	126	149	143	98	122	349	391	349	391	349	391	349	391	349	391
Activities	50.3	47.7	50.1	48.4	50.7	50.5	50.3	48.8	7.1	7.5	7.4	6.8	2.3	2.3	.1	.1
Social	45.5	48.9	42.7	48.5	45.0	50.6	44.2	49.3	12.0	7.1	6.0	6.8	2.2	1.8	.1	.1
School[b]	2.0	2.3	2.0	2.3	2.0	2.5	—	—	—	—	2.0	2.3	.6	.5	.0	.0
Total Competence	50.9	50.3	50.6	50.4	50.4	53.8	50.6	51.5	10.8	9.9	15.8	16.1	3.9	3.6	.2	.2
Aggressive	60.9	58.2	62.0	57.8	59.3	56.8	60.9	57.6	7.8	5.0	12.8	9.5	6.4	5.3	.3	.3
Delinquent	62.1	58.4	62.3	57.4	60.2	57.1	61.7	57.6	7.5	5.1	9.3	5.7	6.2	4.6	.3	.2
Depressed	61.4	57.4	62.6	57.1	61.4	56.9	61.9	57.1	8.6	4.3	23.0	15.0	12.7	9.0	.7	.5
Somatic	62.7	58.9	62.3	57.8	59.9	56.2	61.7	57.7	8.6	5.1	8.5	5.6	5.4	3.9	.3	.2
Thought Disorder	65.8	58.8	66.4	58.0	62.9	56.8	65.2	57.9	10.4	5.3	8.7	4.8	4.9	3.2	.3	.2
Unpopular	61.3	57.6	61.9	57.7	59.7	56.6	61.1	57.4	7.5	4.7	6.3	4.2	4.0	3.0	.2	.2
Internalizing	59.0	51.1	59.9	51.7	57.2	49.9	58.8	50.9	12.0	9.8	30.5	20.1	15.8	11.4	.8	.6
Externalizing	58.3	52.4	59.6	51.7	55.9	50.0	58.2	51.4	11.0	10.0	20.1	14.0	10.4	.4	.6	8.2
Total Problems	59.5	51.5	60.7	51.4	56.6	49.0	59.2	50.7	11.7	10.2	64.1	44.0	28.4	1.1	1.5	21.4

[a] Hollingshead (1975) occupational levels 1-3.5 = lower SES; 4-6.5 = middle SES; 7-9 = upper SES.
[b] Raw scores only, because no T scores are computed for the School score.

APPENDIX D

Pearson Correlations Among T Scores for Boys
Referred Sample Above Diagonal, Nonreferred Sample Below Diagonal

	Act.	Soc.	Total Comp.	Agg.	Del.	Dep.	Self-Dest.	Som.	Thot. Dis.	Unpop.	Int.	Ext.	Total Probs.
Activities		15	69	15	10	05	05	06	12	13	14	17	17
Social	27		68	06	-02	-20	-21	-03	01	-20	-19	-03	-12
Total Competence	74	69		14	01	-01	01	14	14	02	-01	05	05
Aggressive	02	-03	-06		74	43	42	37	42	46	49	78	63
Delinquent	-09	-14	-14	75		37	40	36	42	42	47	84	65
Depressed	01	-10	-07	29	30		70	70	37	78	82	44	71
Self Destructive/Identity Probs.	-02	-11	-11	26	29	62		48	40	73	69	44	65
Somatic	09	04	02	34	23	47	48		36	53	57	39	63
Thought Disorder	06	01	07	24	38	40	23	39		48	55	47	66
Unpopular	-01	-13	-12	35	40	69	71	45	36		83	49	73
Internalizing	08	-07	-02	42	40	68	62	47	43	70		64	92
Externalizing	02	-07	-08	72	73	35	35	35	28	41	65		83
Total Problems	08	-05	-03	56	56	60	58	55	48	63	91	83	

Note. $N = 366$ referred, 388 nonreferred; correlations >09 significant at $p<.05$. Decimals omitted.

APPENDIX D (CONT'D)

Pearson Correlations Among T Scores for Girls
Referred Sample Above Diagonal, Nonreferred Sample Below Diagonal

	Act.	Soc.	Total Comp.	Agg.	Del.	Dep.	Som.	Thot. Dis.	Unpop.	Int.	Ext.	Total Probs.
Activities		26	69	-21	-19	-14	-01	-08	-07	-10	-15	-13
Social	36		72	-10	-08	-21	01	-08	-23	-16	-09	-15
Total Competence	79	67		-14	-19	-26	02	-06	-22	-17	-18	-18
Aggressive	00	-12	-07		74	51	42	59	41	53	83	71
Delinquent	-09	-20	-18	70		44	30	57	35	46	87	67
Depressed	01	-14	-05	59	57		57	58	54	86	55	79
Somatic	03	00	-01	34	34	57		56	39	70	41	64
Thought Disorder	-02	-05	-07	50	50	53	42		42	65	67	75
Unpopular	-03	-16	-05	43	50	48	28	31		55	45	63
Internalizing	02	-13	-09	52	48	75	63	51	46		63	92
Externalizing	-04	-17	-14	76	74	59	40	55	47	71		84
Total Problems	02	-14	-08	66	63	71	57	58	57	92	89	

Note. $N = 349$ referred, 391 nonreferred; correlations > 09 significant at $p < .05$. Decimals omitted.

APPENDIX E

Percent of Referred and Nonreferred Adolescents Scoring 1 and 2 on Each Problem and Socially Desirable Item

Item[a]	Group[b]	Age 11-12			Age 13-14			Age 15-16			Age 17-18		
		1	2	Tot[c]	1	2	Tot	1	2	Tot	1	2	Tot
1. Acts too young	RB	49	11	59	39	7	46	34	4	38	36	2	38
	RG	41	11	52	21	5	26	30	6	37	45	2	47
	NB	33	5	38	39	3	42	21	5	26	38	2	40
	NG	35	4	39	33	2	35	31	3	34	19	1	20
2. Allergy	RB	12	19	31	10	24	34	17	13	30	20	18	38
	RG	14	15	30	9	21	30	9	23	32	2	23	25
	NB	11	25	36	9	25	34	14	12	26	13	18	31
	NG	7	30	36	8	21	30	11	16	27	10	17	27
3. Argues a lot	RB	51	39	90	57	34	91	47	32	79	57	17	75
	RG	52	34	87	48	37	85	59	29	87	61	26	87
	NB	58	26	84	62	19	80	52	24	76	58	12	70
	NG	62	22	84	61	24	85	56	25	80	55	22	77
4. Asthma	RB	3	4	7	7	7	14	4	4	8	6	1	7
	RG	3	5	8	3	10	13	4	1	5	4	5	9
	NB	5	10	15	7	4	11	5	6	11	3	5	8
	NG	2	6	8	3	4	6	2	7	9	1	4	5

[a]See the YSR for actual wording of items; soc. des. indicates socially desirable items.
[b]RB = referred boys; RG = referred girls; NB = nonreferred boys; NG = nonreferred girls.
[c]Tot indicates total percent for whom the problem was reported to be present; sum of 1s and 2s may not equal total due to rounding.

APPENDIX E (CONT'D)

Percent of Referred and Nonreferred Adolescents Scoring 1 and 2 on Each Problem and Socially Desirable Item

Item[a]	Group[b]	Age 11-12			Age 13-14			Age 15-16			Age 17-18		
		1	2	Tot	1	2	Tot	1	2	Tot	1	2	Tot
5. Acts like opposite sex	RB	4	3	7	3	5	8	1	6	7	5	3	7
	RG	15	6	21	18	10	28	16	5	21	13	13	26
	NB	1	4	5	1	5	6	5	8	13	2	7	9
	NG	16	4	20	16	4	20	19	8	26	12	3	16
6. Likes animals (soc. des.)	RB	16	78	94	25	69	94	22	71	93	21	68	88
	RG	10	85	95	15	77	92	19	76	95	32	64	96
	NB	16	80	96	26	68	95	26	64	90	36	52	88
	NG	14	82	96	25	71	96	26	64	91	22	66	88
7. Brags	RB	47	15	63	44	5	49	47	4	52	48	3	51
	RG	41	6	48	34	8	42	35	2	37	33	14	46
	NB	36	2	39	53	4	57	38	4	42	46	4	50
	NG	42	1	43	27	7	34	46	2	48	37	5	42
8. Can't concentrate	RB	51	30	82	61	18	79	50	23	74	59	23	82
	RG	45	24	69	51	21	72	46	28	75	48	22	70
	NB	49	12	61	46	14	60	40	16	56	47	8	55
	NG	40	6	46	47	12	60	46	14	59	43	9	52
9. Can't get mind off thoughts	RB	31	27	58	42	18	59	29	26	55	25	42	67
	RG	33	30	64	34	36	70	29	37	66	41	40	81
	NB	17	9	26	13	6	19	15	11	26	15	7	22
	NG	6	5	11	10	5	14	10	4	14	9	8	17

APPENDIX E (CONT'D)

Percent of Referred and Nonreferred Adolescents Scoring 1 and 2 on Each Problem and Socially Desirable Item

Item[a]	Group[b]	Age 11-12			Age 13-14			Age 15-16			Age 17-18		
		1	2	Tot	1	2	Tot	1	2	Tot	1	2	Tot
10. Trouble sitting still	RB	36	32	68	38	20	58	45	16	60	44	21	65
	RG	28	32	60	39	21	61	36	25	61	41	13	54
	NB	46	15	61	45	15	60	35	22	56	40	15	55
	NG	27	10	37	41	10	51	39	18	57	36	9	45
11. Too dependent	RB	38	18	56	32	7	39	30	4	34	29	20	49
	RG	36	13	50	33	8	41	34	10	44	33	18	51
	NB	33	10	43	38	4	42	25	8	33	29	3	32
	NG	36	8	44	33	4	37	25	7	32	38	6	44
12. Lonely	RB	38	10	48	37	7	43	34	13	47	54	8	62
	RG	42	19	60	47	18	65	44	21	66	44	33	77
	NB	23	4	27	27	2	29	23	3	25	28	4	32
	NG	34	2	36	30	8	37	41	9	51	41	6	46
13. Confused	RB	42	10	52	28	10	38	34	11	44	42	13	55
	RG	41	13	54	36	20	56	40	24	64	40	28	68
	NB	31	2	33	22	2	24	20	4	23	20	6	26
	NG	24	1	25	36	5	40	33	6	39	36	7	42
14. Cries	RB	29	11	41	22	5	27	16	3	19	18	3	21
	RG	42	19	61	40	20	60	51	23	74	40	27	67

APPENDIX E (CONT'D)

Percent of Referred and Nonreferred Adolescents Scoring 1 and 2 on Each Problem and Socially Desirable Item

Item[a]	Group[b]	Age 11-12			Age 13-14			Age 15-16			Age 17-18		
		1	2	Tot	1	2	Tot	1	2	Tot	1	2	Tot
	NB	22	2	24	12	1	13	7	0	7	6	0	6
	NG	37	2	39	35	3	38	39	3	42	27	12	39
15. Honest (soc. des.)	RB	65	27	92	67	28	95	43	46	89	47	47	94
	RG	55	32	88	56	35	90	48	44	92	31	65	96
	NB	58	37	95	65	28	93	52	39	91	47	49	96
	NG	49	39	88	57	38	95	46	51	98	34	55	89
16. Mean to others	RB	37	14	51	40	8	48	47	4	51	32	6	38
	RG	45	6	51	33	8	40	38	5	43	46	4	50
	NB	31	0	31	36	1	37	25	1	26	37	0	37
	NG	34	1	35	40	2	42	32	3	35	20	1	21
17. Daydreams	RB	34	22	56	48	15	63	48	19	67	42	26	68
	RG	29	28	57	38	30	69	40	34	74	58	20	78
	NB	34	14	48	40	13	53	39	17	56	43	16	59
	NG	35	9	44	48	14	63	48	24	72	59	19	78
18. Harms self	RB	12	4	16	2	2	4	8	2	11	8	3	11
	RG	11	5	16	19	12	31	21	10	31	24	10	34
	NB	0	0	0	3	1	4	1	0	1	3	0	3
	NG	2	1	3	3	3	6	10	4	13	6	1	7

APPENDIX E (CONT'D)

Percent of Referred and Nonreferred Adolescents Scoring 1 and 2 on Each Problem and Socially Desirable Item

Item[a]	Group[b]	Age 11-12			Age 13-14			Age 15-16			Age 17-18		
		1	2	Tot	1	2	Tot	1	2	Tot	1	2	Tot
19. Tries to get attention	RB	37	22	59	40	10	50	48	15	63	61	7	68
	RG	41	18	59	38	13	52	46	14	60	38	16	54
	NB	42	10	52	55	8	63	31	6	37	35	6	41
	NG	40	8	48	43	8	51	32	8	41	43	5	48
20. Destroys own things	RB	37	8	45	28	10	38	24	1	25	12	7	19
	RG	24	4	28	24	3	26	17	3	20	20	5	26
	NB	16	2	18	10	4	14	9	2	11	11	6	17
	NG	9	2	11	15	2	17	10	2	12	8	1	9
21. Destroys others' things	RB	16	6	22	20	2	22	22	1	22	12	4	16
	RG	6	4	10	13	7	20	11	2	13	16	5	21
	NB	13	2	15	13	1	14	5	3	8	11	3	14
	NG	7	1	8	8	1	9	5	0	5	2	0	2
22. Disobeys parents	RB	57	13	70	52	10	62	54	16	69	46	11	57
	RG	57	14	71	49	21	70	60	14	74	59	5	64
	NB	44	4	48	55	2	57	47	3	50	55	5	60
	NG	50	1	51	59	3	62	49	7	56	59	4	63
23. Disobeys at school	RB	50	13	63	50	13	63	45	16	61	54	11	64
	RG	30	6	36	28	16	44	29	12	41	40	8	48

APPENDIX E (CONT'D)

Percent of Referred and Nonreferred Adolescents Scoring 1 and 2 on Each Problem and Socially Desirable Item

Item[a]	Group[b]	Age 11-12			Age 13-14			Age 15-16			Age 17-18		
		1	2	Tot	1	2	Tot	1	2	Tot	1	2	Tot
	NB	34	1	35	45	5	50	36	4	40	32	3	35
	NG	21	2	23	30	4	34	26	5	32	33	2	35
24. Doesn't eat well	RB	26	18	44	24	11	35	36	20	56	29	13	42
	RG	30	15	46	30	24	54	29	28	57	29	29	57
	NB	22	13	35	26	8	34	28	7	34	39	13	52
	NG	31	11	43	40	21	61	37	30	67	44	19	63
25. Doesn't get along	RB	38	16	54	38	11	49	34	4	38	41	9	50
	RG	40	10	50	33	9	42	30	15	45	51	10	60
	NB	29	0	29	30	1	31	13	1	14	22	0	22
	NG	19	1	20	22	2	24	17	2	20	17	2	19
26. Lacks guilt	RB	38	21	59	41	18	59	42	8	50	38	10	48
	RG	34	21	55	33	14	47	38	9	47	34	15	49
	NB	29	13	41	32	12	44	41	9	50	43	12	55
	NG	21	21	42	37	11	48	23	14	37	33	11	44
27. Jealous	RB	31	5	36	31	7	38	38	6	44	35	11	46
	RG	38	10	47	40	12	53	45	12	57	51	11	62
	NB	34	2	37	52	1	53	33	3	36	38	9	47
	NG	34	6	40	54	5	59	41	7	48	52	7	59

APPENDIX E (CONT'D)

Percent of Referred and Nonreferred Adolescents Scoring 1 and 2 on Each Problem and Socially Desirable Item

Item[a]	Group[b]	Age 11-12			Age 13-14			Age 15-16			Age 17-18		
		1	2	Tot	1	2	Tot	1	2	Tot	1	2	Tot
28. Willing to help (soc. des.)	RB	34	54	88	44	48	92	43	53	96	29	57	86
	RG	34	61	95	29	63	93	28	65	93	29	68	97
	NB	39	49	88	41	57	98	31	58	89	36	56	92
	NG	24	64	88	27	69	96	21	75	96	17	79	96
29. Fears	RB	33	24	57	29	15	44	28	12	40	30	19	49
	RG	22	25	47	33	26	59	27	24	51	25	40	64
	NB	34	17	51	35	23	58	25	15	40	27	17	43
	NG	28	31	59	34	26	60	25	19	44	21	26	47
30. Fears school	RB	11	3	14	15	5	20	11	4	15	16	2	18
	RG	16	10	26	19	6	25	17	9	26	29	6	35
	NB	13	3	16	11	3	14	12	1	13	13	2	15
	NG	14	3	17	19	3	22	10	1	11	6	4	10
31. Fears impulses	RB	34	10	44	29	10	39	29	6	35	27	15	42
	RG	36	12	48	21	16	36	27	11	38	26	18	44
	NB	40	4	44	30	7	37	18	4	22	24	3	27
	NG	29	5	34	31	3	34	23	5	28	20	5	24
32. Needs to be perfect	RB	22	15	37	31	16	47	31	16	47	42	14	56
	RG	38	21	59	39	13	53	41	18	59	39	20	58

APPENDIX E (CONT'D)

Percent of Referred and Nonreferred Adolescents Scoring 1 and 2 on Each Problem and Socially Desirable Item

Item[a]	Group[b]	Age 11-12			Age 13-14			Age 15-16			Age 17-18		
		1	2	Tot	1	2	Tot	1	2	Tot	1	2	Tot
	NB	32	6	38	31	11	42	35	7	42	41	5	45
	NG	33	13	46	35	8	43	41	17	57	28	16	44
33. Feels unloved	RB	30	7	37	21	2	23	19	5	23	29	6	35
	RG	35	17	52	39	7	46	38	9	48	39	15	54
	NB	20	3	23	16	2	18	7	1	8	11	2	13
	NG	20	2	22	21	4	24	21	5	27	20	2	22
34. Feels persecuted	RB	30	12	42	28	4	32	38	6	44	24	7	31
	RG	29	9	38	34	13	48	29	14	43	37	16	53
	NB	22	1	23	22	4	26	14	2	16	21	3	24
	NG	20	3	23	25	4	29	23	7	30	16	4	21
35. Feels worthless	RB	29	9	38	21	6	27	19	4	22	21	14	35
	RG	33	15	48	26	14	40	35	16	51	29	23	52
	NB	17	2	19	16	0	16	14	0	14	15	1	16
	NG	16	1	17	18	7	25	21	6	27	27	2	29
36. Accident-prone	RB	38	22	60	33	15	47	30	8	38	24	10	34
	RG	32	12	44	26	14	40	23	11	34	23	14	38
	NB	35	13	47	34	10	44	24	12	37	19	3	21
	NG	30	10	40	19	7	26	20	7	28	20	8	28

APPENDIX E (CONT'D)

Percent of Referred and Nonreferred Adolescents Scoring 1 and 2 on Each Problem and Socially Desirable Item

Item[a]	Group[b]	Age 11-12			Age 13-14			Age 15-16			Age 17-18		
		1	2	Tot	1	2	Tot	1	2	Tot	1	2	Tot
37. Fighting	RB	37	25	62	40	6	45	29	6	36	20	6	26
	RG	31	9	40	31	15	47	26	10	36	30	4	34
	NB	41	6	47	32	6	38	19	9	28	19	6	25
	NG	19	6	25	17	3	20	15	5	21	17	2	19
38. Is teased	RB	33	36	69	38	16	54	32	7	39	28	9	37
	RG	36	32	68	28	17	45	21	16	37	29	16	46
	NB	40	6	46	33	4	37	19	7	26	15	4	18
	NG	22	9	31	31	8	39	23	9	33	17	7	23
39. Hangs around kids who get in trouble	RB	39	17	56	33	25	58	50	17	66	32	15	47
	RG	34	10	44	27	28	54	31	18	49	41	8	48
	NB	37	10	47	39	12	50	32	13	44	34	13	48
	NG	26	4	30	30	8	38	40	6	46	23	6	29
40. Hears things	RB	23	12	35	16	3	19	14	6	20	23	8	31
	RG	20	14	34	20	9	29	13	10	23	11	9	19
	NB	10	2	12	9	2	11	11	1	12	11	3	14
	NG	5	1	6	5	3	8	3	0	3	3	2	6
41. Acts without thinking	RB	48	25	73	48	25	73	46	23	69	53	10	64
	RG	53	19	73	50	23	73	65	17	82	58	26	83

APPENDIX E (CONT'D)

Percent of Referred and Nonreferred Adolescents Scoring 1 and 2 on Each Problem and Socially Desirable Item

Item[a]	Group[b]	Age 11-12			Age 13-14			Age 15-16			Age 17-18		
		1	2	Tot	1	2	Tot	1	2	Tot	1	2	Tot
	NB	56	12	68	61	8	68	57	9	66	55	5	60
	NG	40	11	51	66	10	76	61	11	73	61	11	73
42. Likes to be alone	RB	48	23	72	56	16	72	61	22	84	44	38	82
	RG	59	24	82	48	24	72	55	33	88	54	26	80
	NB	58	8	66	54	12	66	45	16	61	56	12	68
	NG	54	14	69	65	14	79	63	24	86	67	11	78
43. Lying or cheating	RB	45	7	53	46	3	49	48	2	49	35	1	36
	RG	39	10	49	38	1	40	45	5	49	36	9	45
	NB	32	2	34	40	1	41	33	1	34	32	3	35
	NG	29	3	32	38	2	39	26	1	27	31	0	31
44. Bites fingernails	RB	26	37	63	27	35	63	26	39	65	30	24	54
	RG	37	35	72	21	51	73	28	33	61	29	35	64
	NB	27	27	54	28	23	51	30	26	56	23	19	42
	NG	27	41	68	31	32	63	20	25	45	31	14	45
45. Nervous	RB	35	17	52	37	17	53	48	14	62	46	16	62
	RG	37	24	62	38	31	70	45	32	78	53	27	80
	NB	45	6	51	33	2	35	33	8	42	37	5	42
	NG	39	7	46	51	4	55	43	12	56	57	10	67

APPENDIX E (CONT'D)

Percent of Referred and Nonreferred Adolescents Scoring 1 and 2 on Each Problem and Socially Desirable Item

Item[a]	Group[b]	Age 11-12			Age 13-14			Age 15-16			Age 17-18		
		1	2	Tot	1	2	Tot	1	2	Tot	1	2	Tot
46. Nervous movements	RB	28	9	37	20	13	33	18	5	23	20	19	39
	RG	23	14	37	24	16	40	27	16	43	23	20	43
	NB	17	5	22	10	1	11	15	11	25	21	5	26
	NG	20	3	23	19	6	25	20	6	26	19	5	23
47. Nightmares	RB	34	20	54	32	7	39	29	9	38	29	6	35
	RG	36	20	56	40	14	55	36	12	49	34	17	51
	NB	43	8	51	35	0	35	22	6	28	18	4	22
	NG	44	4	48	46	4	50	41	6	47	39	6	45
48. Not liked	RB	39	13	52	40	5	45	35	4	38	33	2	36
	RG	34	14	48	31	8	38	30	11	41	41	13	53
	NB	22	3	25	24	1	25	12	2	15	15	4	19
	NG	21	6	28	34	0	34	20	0	20	15	3	19
49. Can do things better (soc. des.)	RB	43	39	82	52	33	85	49	30	79	50	37	87
	RG	47	32	79	56	26	81	48	30	78	48	29	76
	NB	48	31	79	53	31	84	48	40	88	53	30	83
	NG	47	27	74	57	20	77	63	15	78	48	28	76
50. Fearful or anxious	RB	34	17	51	31	8	39	29	9	39	42	15	57
	RG	36	12	48	22	12	34	35	17	52	25	23	48

APPENDIX E (CONT'D)

Percent of Referred and Nonreferred Adolescents Scoring 1 and 2 on Each Problem and Socially Desirable Item

Item[a]	Group[b]	Age 11-12			Age 13-14			Age 15-16			Age 17-18		
		1	2	Tot	1	2	Tot	1	2	Tot	1	2	Tot
	NB	33	4	37	18	4	21	24	4	29	28	2	30
	NG	26	4	31	29	2	31	27	7	34	30	5	35
51. Dizzy	RB	23	10	33	17	4	21	27	2	28	23	4	27
	RG	32	7	39	29	11	40	26	6	32	24	9	33
	NB	21	0	21	16	3	19	13	2	15	10	1	11
	NG	17	3	20	11	3	14	21	5	26	9	1	10
52. Feels too guilty	RB	18	9	28	23	8	31	28	4	32	34	7	42
	RG	34	8	41	22	8	30	31	8	39	31	17	48
	NB	19	0	19	18	1	19	17	2	19	15	2	16
	NG	20	2	22	18	5	23	24	5	29	20	2	22
53. Eats too much	RB	29	20	49	27	19	47	20	13	33	37	5	42
	RG	29	29	58	41	23	64	42	20	62	34	21	54
	NB	37	11	48	43	19	62	22	16	38	31	5	37
	NG	49	9	58	40	22	62	34	22	55	48	10	58
54. Overtired	RB	38	19	57	31	15	46	47	20	67	56	9	65
	RG	49	12	61	45	19	64	36	26	62	55	25	80
	NB	36	4	40	36	9	45	33	14	48	35	13	48
	NG	43	4	47	42	13	55	53	19	73	47	11	58

APPENDIX E (CONT'D)

Percent of Referred and Nonreferred Adolescents Scoring 1 and 2 on Each Problem and Socially Desirable Item

Item[a]	Group[b]	Age 11-12			Age 13-14			Age 15-16			Age 17-18		
		1	2	Tot	1	2	Tot	1	2	Tot	1	2	Tot
55. Overweight	RB	12	17	28	12	5	17	10	5	15	12	6	19
	RG	21	20	41	22	28	50	21	32	53	17	26	43
	NB	16	4	20	13	9	22	9	1	10	17	6	23
	NG	15	8	23	16	18	35	20	17	36	27	15	42
56a. Aches or pains	RB	40	12	52	29	7	36	17	9	27	29	6	35
	RG	43	11	53	29	12	41	27	12	39	32	12	44
	NB	34	2	36	25	4	29	16	2	18	15	2	17
	NG	13	5	19	26	4	30	38	8	46	15	8	23
56b. Headaches	RB	37	19	56	37	9	46	35	12	47	23	4	27
	RG	45	19	64	39	24	62	39	25	64	58	7	65
	NB	33	10	44	28	6	34	25	5	30	18	1	19
	NG	34	4	38	33	16	49	41	11	52	33	13	46
56c. Nausea, feels sick	RB	35	10	45	22	8	30	20	2	22	10	5	15
	RG	39	12	51	28	9	38	23	14	37	29	12	40
	NB	15	6	21	16	0	16	13	2	15	5	1	6
	NG	18	0	18	19	5	25	23	3	26	15	3	18

APPENDIX E (CONT'D)

Percent of Referred and Nonreferred Adolescents Scoring 1 and 2 on Each Problem and Socially Desirable Item

Item[a]	Group[b]	Age 11-12			Age 13-14			Age 15-16			Age 17-18		
		1	2	Tot	1	2	Tot	1	2	Tot	1	2	Tot
56d. Eye problems	RB	21	7	29	16	9	26	13	10	23	11	8	18
	RG	21	15	35	17	12	29	20	12	32	16	0	16
	NB	10	7	17	9	3	12	7	4	10	7	2	9
	NG	4	7	11	10	4	14	14	7	21	7	3	10
56e. Skin problems	RB	21	5	26	15	9	24	12	3	16	24	4	28
	RG	20	6	26	16	13	29	13	7	20	23	2	25
	NB	12	3	15	18	3	21	9	5	14	15	3	18
	NG	11	8	20	15	9	24	17	11	28	11	7	18
56f. Stomachaches	RB	38	18	57	30	9	39	21	3	24	18	11	28
	RG	43	17	60	43	15	58	35	21	55	54	12	66
	NB	33	4	37	26	3	29	23	4	28	13	2	15
	NG	25	5	30	34	9	42	40	14	54	24	9	33
56g. Vomiting	RB	23	8	31	18	0	18	8	1	9	7	0	7
	RG	28	4	32	14	4	19	15	2	16	15	3	18
	NB	12	1	13	9	0	9	13	1	14	6	0	6
	NG	13	1	14	9	3	12	9	2	11	9	2	11
56h. Other physical problems	RB	7	5	12	3	0	3	3	1	4	4	2	6
	RG	4	11	14	4	6	10	0	1	1	3	0	3
	NB	1	1	2	4	3	7	3	1	4	0	0	0
	NG	3	6	9	3	1	4	1	3	5	3	0	3

APPENDIX E (CONT'D)

Percent of Referred and Nonreferred Adolescents Scoring 1 and 2 on Each Problem and Socially Desirable Item

Item[a]	Group[b]	Age 11-12			Age 13-14			Age 15-16			Age 17-18		
		1	2	Tot	1	2	Tot	1	2	Tot	1	2	Tot
57. Attacks people	RB	17	7	24	19	2	20	18	3	21	18	3	21
	RG	13	0	13	15	6	20	22	1	22	20	0	20
	NB	6	1	7	9	0	9	10	2	12	10	1	11
	NG	2	1	3	9	3	12	9	2	11	10	0	10
58. Picking	RB	21	11	33	17	9	26	13	0	13	27	2	29
	RG	19	12	31	13	9	22	18	5	23	15	6	21
	NB	13	4	17	19	5	24	11	5	16	20	1	21
	NG	20	2	22	15	5	20	16	1	17	5	1	6
59. Friendly (soc. des.)	RB	34	59	93	41	53	94	32	66	98	33	63	96
	RG	28	70	98	31	62	93	30	69	99	23	74	97
	NB	35	61	96	40	56	96	27	66	92	30	64	94
	NG	32	66	98	30	66	96	18	79	98	22	72	94
60. Likes new things (soc. des.)	RB	24	69	93	32	56	88	33	59	92	30	59	89
	RG	40	55	96	34	55	89	39	53	92	41	56	96
	NB	27	64	91	44	53	97	25	67	93	51	47	98
	NG	30	62	92	37	57	94	29	69	98	27	65	92
61. Poor school work	RB	40	19	59	47	11	58	32	20	52	57	9	66
	RG	39	16	55	27	21	47	28	22	50	48	12	60
	NB	33	3	36	39	5	44	27	12	39	43	3	46
	NG	28	1	29	32	5	37	29	11	40	32	4	36

APPENDIX E (CONT'D)

Percent of Referred and Nonreferred Adolescents Scoring 1 and 2 on Each Problem and Socially Desirable Item

Item[a]	Group[b]	Age 11-12			Age 13-14			Age 15-16			Age 17-18		
		1	2	Tot	1	2	Tot	1	2	Tot	1	2	Tot
62. Clumsy	RB	33	12	45	23	4	27	23	2	24	20	2	23
	RG	32	4	36	23	6	30	15	8	23	36	3	40
	NB	24	3	27	17	0	17	14	2	17	11	3	14
	NG	17	3	20	17	4	21	20	4	24	15	6	21
63. Prefers older kids	RB	28	21	49	41	22	62	44	26	70	35	24	59
	RG	31	20	50	41	29	69	33	44	77	44	42	86
	NB	31	7	38	47	8	55	42	18	60	44	12	56
	NG	33	11	44	48	10	58	52	16	68	39	26	65
64. Prefers younger kids	RB	26	10	36	22	3	25	24	3	27	29	12	41
	RG	27	11	37	17	7	24	12	2	14	19	3	22
	NB	22	3	25	16	1	17	18	2	20	15	3	18
	NG	17	7	24	14	4	17	11	1	12	16	0	16
65. Refuses to talk	RB	33	10	43	40	3	43	42	2	44	32	7	38
	RG	30	6	36	43	10	53	36	9	45	52	8	60
	NB	19	3	22	21	1	22	18	2	20	17	3	20
	NG	24	2	26	18	4	23	27	5	32	18	2	20
66. Repeats actions	RB	18	10	29	28	7	34	19	5	24	27	6	33
	RG	29	13	42	19	14	33	14	14	27	18	14	32
	NB	18	0	18	11	2	14	11	1	12	11	2	13
	NG	6	2	8	11	1	12	14	1	15	11	0	11

APPENDIX E (CONT'D)

Percent of Referred and Nonreferred Adolescents Scoring 1 and 2 on Each Problem and Socially Desirable Item

Item[a]	Group[b]	Age 11-12			Age 13-14			Age 15-16			Age 17-18		
		1	2	Tot	1	2	Tot	1	2	Tot	1	2	Tot
67. Runs away from home	RB	12	7	19	16	5	21	19	4	23	19	3	22
	RG	12	5	17	19	13	32	22	10	32	30	13	43
	NB	4	0	4	4	0	4	2	2	4	4	1	5
	NG	3	1	4	4	2	6	11	6	17	3	3	7
68. Screams a lot	RB	29	9	38	31	7	38	13	5	18	19	3	21
	RG	37	15	52	30	25	55	34	12	46	26	19	45
	NB	19	2	21	17	2	20	12	5	17	13	1	14
	NG	23	4	27	33	8	41	30	12	42	28	4	32
69. Secretive	RB	43	29	72	42	24	66	43	30	73	34	42	76
	RG	49	27	76	36	47	83	45	37	82	52	38	90
	NB	50	10	61	47	12	59	43	16	58	49	19	67
	NG	44	11	54	64	16	80	47	27	74	51	23	74
70. Sees things	RB	8	14	22	10	6	16	12	6	18	13	4	17
	RG	18	13	32	10	10	20	7	12	19	13	8	21
	NB	5	3	8	7	1	8	6	4	10	10	2	12
	NG	6	2	8	5	1	6	6	2	8	3	3	7
71. Self-conscious	RB	37	17	54	43	10	53	41	18	58	42	17	59
	RG	42	29	71	46	23	69	43	35	77	32	47	79
	NB	49	7	56	47	9	55	37	13	50	36	13	48
	NG	42	15	57	50	24	73	46	27	73	56	20	76

APPENDIX E (CONT'D)

Percent of Referred and Nonreferred Adolescents Scoring 1 and 2 on Each Problem and Socially Desirable Item

Item[a]	Group[b]	Age 11-12			Age 13-14			Age 15-16			Age 17-18		
		1	2	Tot	1	2	Tot	1	2	Tot	1	2	Tot
72. Sets fires	RB	15	7	22	14	4	18	9	2	11	3	4	7
	RG	5	0	5	3	2	5	4	1	5	5	0	5
	NB	5	1	6	12	1	13	5	3	8	3	0	3
	NG	3	0	3	6	1	7	2	1	3	0	0	0
73. Works well with hands (soc. des.)	RB	38	55	93	39	45	84	42	49	90	34	47	81
	RG	42	43	85	43	42	85	42	29	71	45	47	92
	NB	40	45	85	41	48	89	36	55	90	45	41	86
	NG	43	35	78	49	29	78	56	22	79	48	33	81
74. Shows off	RB	41	14	54	50	7	57	50	9	59	54	12	66
	RG	40	7	47	35	6	41	26	8	33	32	6	38
	NB	38	3	41	47	7	54	44	6	51	39	11	50
	NG	29	4	33	29	4	33	35	10	44	31	3	34
75. Shy	RB	33	13	46	35	14	49	46	12	58	41	14	55
	RG	42	19	61	41	13	54	44	22	67	40	32	72
	NB	38	13	51	31	10	41	37	11	48	38	8	46
	NG	46	19	65	49	16	64	39	19	58	51	10	61
76. Sleeps little	RB	32	23	55	28	13	41	33	19	52	25	13	38
	RG	31	25	56	31	20	51	22	16	38	35	12	47
	NB	39	13	52	33	14	47	18	13	31	34	10	44
	NG	18	7	25	16	11	27	38	13	51	22	8	30

APPENDIX E (CONT'D)

Percent of Referred and Nonreferred Adolescents Scoring 1 and 2 on Each Problem and Socially Desirable Item

Item[a]	Group[b]	Age 11-12			Age 13-14			Age 15-16			Age 17-18		
		1	2	Tot	1	2	Tot	1	2	Tot	1	2	Tot
77. Sleeps much	RB	18	23	41	32	14	47	30	9	39	33	13	46
	RG	16	12	28	29	12	41	22	15	37	40	22	62
	NB	21	4	25	17	9	26	27	14	41	19	9	28
	NG	14	10	24	14	12	26	19	10	29	25	9	34
78. Good imagination (soc. des.)	RB	30	58	88	31	46	77	36	50	86	40	51	91
	RG	44	43	87	42	44	86	36	47	83	40	48	89
	NB	42	47	89	44	47	91	41	52	93	45	42	86
	NG	53	38	91	51	36	87	53	31	84	43	45	88
79. Speech problem	RB	9	10	19	19	3	22	10	4	14	11	3	14
	RG	9	10	19	12	3	15	4	4	8	10	3	13
	NB	9	2	11	6	3	9	7	1	8	7	2	9
	NG	5	1	6	4	5	9	2	0	2	4	0	4
80. Stands up for rights (soc. des.)	RB	32	55	87	35	54	89	33	60	93	38	57	95
	RG	44	40	84	45	46	91	39	49	88	38	52	90
	NB	44	44	88	42	52	94	38	56	95	44	49	93
	NG	48	41	88	49	46	95	40	52	92	39	52	91
81. Steals at home	RB	20	4	24	20	3	23	16	3	19	8	1	9
	RG	11	9	20	10	3	13	9	5	14	16	3	19
	NB	11	1	12	5	1	6	4	0	4	7	0	7
	NG	4	0	4	6	3	9	6	0	6	7	0	7

APPENDIX E (CONT'D)

Percent of Referred and Nonreferred Adolescents Scoring 1 and 2 on Each Problem and Socially Desirable Item

Item[a]	Group[b]	Age 11-12			Age 13-14			Age 15-16			Age 17-18		
		1	2	Tot	1	2	Tot	1	2	Tot	1	2	Tot
82. Steals outside home	RB	13	5	18	18	2	20	18	1	19	18	5	24
	RG	12	2	14	11	0	11	14	3	17	16	1	17
	NB	7	1	8	7	2	9	7	2	9	9	0	9
	NG	1	0	1	3	4	7	7	1	7	8	0	8
83. Stores up unneeded things	RB	24	20	44	35	17	53	31	14	44	43	21	64
	RG	31	28	59	28	27	54	22	21	43	26	26	52
	NB	30	9	39	24	13	37	16	14	30	14	10	24
	NG	20	19	39	26	14	40	19	22	41	18	12	30
84. Strange behavior	RB	24	12	36	28	11	39	32	10	42	23	17	40
	RG	29	11	40	29	17	46	23	18	40	31	16	46
	NB	19	0	19	13	2	14	14	13	27	18	0	18
	NG	13	3	16	15	4	19	19	6	25	5	6	11
85. Strange thoughts	RB	20	11	31	23	7	30	26	11	37	34	16	49
	RG	20	15	35	25	14	39	16	16	33	28	15	43
	NB	16	3	19	23	4	27	12	9	21	14	4	18
	NG	10	5	15	11	5	16	15	8	22	8	7	15
86. Stubborn	RB	50	15	65	49	17	66	50	21	71	47	25	72
	RG	46	21	66	47	34	81	44	39	82	39	27	66
	NB	46	3	49	51	8	59	33	19	52	52	20	72
	NG	44	7	51	55	26	81	52	32	84	55	31	86

APPENDIX E (CONT'D)

Percent of Referred and Nonreferred Adolescents Scoring 1 and 2 on Each Problem and Socially Desirable Item

Item[a]	Group[b]	Age 11-12			Age 13-14			Age 15-16			Age 17-18		
		1	2	Tot	1	2	Tot	1	2	Tot	1	2	Tot
87. Moody	RB	37	22	58	32	21	52	43	22	66	50	21	71
	RG	52	23	75	47	35	82	30	47	77	43	47	90
	NB	42	10	52	38	6	43	32	20	53	40	17	57
	NG	30	11	41	40	19	60	47	27	74	46	24	70
88. Enjoys others (soc. des.)	RB	37	59	96	46	46	92	36	61	96	41	55	95
	RG	36	60	97	31	66	97	35	60	96	31	67	99
	NB	32	62	94	38	62	100	18	75	93	33	65	98
	NG	23	72	95	30	70	100	24	74	98	20	76	96
89. Suspicious	RB	32	22	54	42	13	55	56	12	67	42	15	57
	RG	42	17	59	41	14	55	43	16	59	50	16	66
	NB	47	12	59	39	13	52	44	10	54	41	7	48
	NG	41	10	51	48	9	56	36	12	48	49	8	57
90. Swearing	RB	40	19	59	59	17	76	57	20	77	57	30	87
	RG	38	14	52	55	20	74	51	23	74	49	22	71
	NB	40	4	44	55	13	68	55	15	71	63	19	82
	NG	31	0	31	51	9	60	54	13	67	66	7	74
91. Suicidal thoughts	RB	18	6	23	11	3	14	17	0	17	8	15	23
	RG	17	6	23	32	7	39	28	12	40	21	19	40
	NB	7	1	8	5	3	8	8	0	8	6	0	6
	NG	6	1	7	14	5	19	18	4	22	14	0	14

APPENDIX E (CONT'D)

Percent of Referred and Nonreferred Adolescents Scoring 1 and 2 on Each Problem and Socially Desirable Item

Item[a]	Group[b]	Age 11-12			Age 13-14			Age 15-16			Age 17-18		
		1	2	Tot	1	2	Tot	1	2	Tot	1	2	Tot
92. Likes to make others laugh (soc. des.)	RB	40	52	92	49	35	83	38	54	92	33	58	91
	RG	26	64	90	38	47	85	35	55	90	56	42	98
	NB	46	46	92	47	48	95	32	56	88	38	52	90
	NG	33	60	93	35	59	94	30	60	91	27	67	94
93. Talks too much	RB	37	24	61	35	17	52	41	10	50	44	9	53
	RG	39	34	73	49	30	79	52	25	77	39	30	69
	NB	50	7	57	55	9	64	44	20	64	44	12	55
	NG	48	20	68	53	29	82	45	35	80	52	20	72
94. Teases a lot	RB	34	14	48	42	6	48	49	4	53	34	7	41
	RG	38	5	43	28	8	36	27	5	32	37	12	49
	NB	38	3	41	41	8	50	43	3	46	36	7	43
	NG	28	2	30	32	6	39	33	8	42	31	8	38
95. Hot temper	RB	40	39	79	37	35	73	33	33	66	35	28	63
	RG	38	29	67	30	50	81	36	42	78	32	46	78
	NB	33	20	53	37	26	63	37	29	66	41	18	60
	NG	34	16	49	44	23	67	39	30	68	42	26	68
96. Thinks about sex	RB	22	14	36	36	10	46	25	22	48	35	23	57
	RG	12	6	18	29	14	43	29	9	38	31	7	39
	NB	18	3	21	32	18	50	38	13	51	47	15	61
	NG	7	3	10	17	4	21	27	9	36	31	3	35

APPENDIX E (CONT'D)

Percent of Referred and Nonreferred Adolescents Scoring 1 and 2 on Each Problem and Socially Desirable Item

Item[a]	Group[b]	Age 11-12			Age 13-14			Age 15-16			Age 17-18		
		1	2	Tot	1	2	Tot	1	2	Tot	1	2	Tot
97. Threatens people	RB	28	12	40	41	7	48	41	5	47	29	10	39
	RG	23	4	27	27	8	35	22	5	27	39	8	47
	NB	17	4	21	25	4	29	18	4	22	22	4	27
	NG	11	1	12	18	1	19	17	5	22	15	1	17
98. Likes to help (soc. des.)	RB	31	52	82	47	43	90	43	52	95	41	51	92
	RG	34	62	96	35	58	93	29	62	92	24	69	94
	NB	41	50	91	53	44	97	43	46	90	48	43	91
	NG	29	64	93	34	63	97	28	69	97	28	69	97
99. Concerned w. neat & clean	RB	30	27	57	31	25	56	38	21	59	44	17	61
	RG	47	28	75	37	31	68	40	22	62	43	34	76
	NB	39	12	51	50	14	64	48	18	66	38	14	52
	NG	47	22	69	51	24	75	47	31	78	39	24	63
100. Trouble sleeping	RB	22	21	43	30	4	34	28	8	36	23	9	32
	RG	23	25	48	24	25	49	21	24	44	35	14	49
	NB	23	8	31	16	9	25	15	8	22	15	2	17
	NG	15	7	22	22	9	30	29	10	39	24	9	33
101. Truancy	RB	9	9	18	20	7	27	32	8	40	30	13	43
	RG	6	8	14	21	15	35	21	19	40	41	14	54
	NB	8	0	8	8	2	10	21	6	28	26	13	39
	NG	3	0	3	13	6	19	25	2	27	32	4	36

APPENDIX E (CONT'D)

Percent of Referred and Nonreferred Adolescents Scoring 1 and 2 on Each Problem and Socially Desirable Item

Item[a]	Group[b]	Age 11-12			Age 13-14			Age 15-16			Age 17-18		
		1	2	Tot	1	2	Tot	1	2	Tot	1	2	Tot
102. Lacks energy	RB	23	13	36	21	7	28	29	9	37	30	11	40
	RG	31	7	37	41	7	48	35	14	49	44	11	55
	NB	23	3	26	26	4	30	17	4	20	24	5	29
	NG	19	8	27	32	7	39	38	5	43	42	7	48
103. Unhappy, sad, or depressed	RB	41	8	49	30	6	36	45	10	55	36	11	46
	RG	50	15	64	44	19	63	39	31	71	50	25	75
	NB	24	2	26	25	0	25	14	2	17	27	2	28
	NG	26	2	28	37	3	41	35	9	44	45	6	51
104. Loud	RB	34	21	55	39	9	48	27	12	39	22	10	33
	RG	39	13	52	37	20	57	28	11	39	27	11	39
	NB	36	5	41	32	5	37	28	12	40	25	2	27
	NG	30	5	35	39	12	51	28	13	41	29	7	36
105. Alcohol, drugs	RB	5	6	11	18	3	21	23	15	39	34	15	50
	RG	3	2	5	12	12	25	21	12	32	42	11	53
	NB	1	0	1	10	2	12	28	2	30	29	9	39
	NG	1	0	1	8	1	9	19	4	23	29	10	39
106. Fair to others (soc. des.)	RB	44	51	95	57	35	92	41	50	91	37	54	91
	RG	49	48	98	47	48	95	43	52	95	36	62	98
	NB	47	42	89	56	35	91	51	42	93	50	40	90
	NG	32	58	90	40	54	94	33	62	95	34	59	93

APPENDIX E (CONT'D)

Percent of Referred and Nonreferred Adolescents Scoring 1 and 2 on Each Problem and Socially Desirable Item

Item[a]	Group[b]	Age 11-12			Age 13-14			Age 15-16			Age 17-18		
		1	2	Tot	1	2	Tot	1	2	Tot	1	2	Tot
107. Enjoys jokes (soc. des.)	RB	25	70	95	30	61	91	32	62	94	35	60	95
	RG	30	66	96	34	63	96	25	73	98	35	64	99
	NB	21	72	93	19	80	99	15	80	95	25	70	95
	NG	23	75	98	22	77	99	17	81	98	16	83	99
108. Takes life easy (soc. des.)	RB	36	48	84	41	43	84	39	57	95	34	48	82
	RG	43	37	81	42	47	89	36	47	83	36	53	89
	NB	39	42	81	42	49	91	38	54	92	44	48	92
	NG	50	45	95	51	42	93	46	47	93	38	54	92
109. Tries to help (soc. des.)	RB	36	55	91	43	45	88	43	52	95	60	35	95
	RG	33	64	97	38	61	99	43	52	95	20	77	97
	NB	37	53	90	50	45	95	35	57	92	46	50	96
	NG	28	71	99	31	68	99	27	71	98	19	75	95
110. Wishes to be opposite sex	RB	4	3	7	5	1	6	1	1	1	2	0	2
	RG	11	0	11	14	3	17	11	4	15	18	3	21
	NB	1	1	2	2	0	2	5	0	5	2	0	2
	NG	15	1	16	12	2	14	10	5	15	8	0	8
111. Keeps from getting involved	RB	47	17	65	47	9	56	45	12	57	43	11	54
	RG	52	16	68	36	15	51	52	11	63	59	17	77
	NB	45	6	51	48	6	54	38	5	43	42	4	46
	NG	38	11	49	34	10	44	35	7	42	41	8	49

APPENDIX E (CONT'D)

Percent of Referred and Nonreferred Adolescents Scoring 1 and 2 on Each Problem and Socially Desirable Item

Item[a]	Group[b]	Age 11-12			Age 13-14			Age 15-16			Age 17-18		
		1	2	Tot[c]	1	2	Tot	1	2	Tot	1	2	Tot
112. Worries a lot	RB	37	27	63	34	16	49	37	12	50	37	26	63
	RG	34	38	73	30	36	65	40	43	83	32	46	78
	NB	37	6	43	37	5	42	30	11	41	34	10	44
	NG	33	12	45	56	17	73	31	31	62	47	18	65

INDEX

Abramowitz, M., 12, 24, 166
abuse, physical & sexual, 141, 151
academic achievement, 118-9, 126, 163
Achenbach, T.M., 1, 7, 12, 19, 22, 24, 31, 38, 40, 43, 46, 61, 70, 107, 117, 119, 129, 144, 163, 166-7
Activities scale, 10, 72-3, 160, 162
adult disorders, 148
age differences, 47-8, 69-70
Aggressive scale, 19
agreement between raters, 1
Akkerhuis, G.W., 70, 144, 166-7
Althaus, M., 20, 167
American Psychiatric Association, 46, 137, 167
anxiety, 127-8
Armenakis, A.A., 39, 167

Baron, G.D., 20, 70, 144, 167
Beall, G., 39, 47, 62, 168
broad-band groupings & scales, 31-5, 52

can't get mind off thoughts (item 9), 56, 73-4, 158
case examples, 13, 22-4, 121-9, 133-5
Child Behavior Checklist (CBCL) & Profile, 1, 14, 19-21, 39, 40, 43-7, 72-7, 107-13, 144
classification, 54
clinicians' ratings, 40
cluster analysis, 164
cognitive assessment, 118
Cohen, B.H., 39, 47, 62, 168
Cohen, J., 47, 63, 70, 73, 167

Compas, B.E., 42, 107, 109, 111-2
competence scores, 10-3, 47-9, 62-3, 69-70, 72-3, 160, 162
computer scoring, 10, 56, 161, 169
confidentiality, 115, 136
correlations between raters, 1, 107-111
Costello, A.J., 138, 167
cutoff scores, 51-9, 160

Delinquent scale, 20, 50
Depressed scale & depressive affect, 20, 22, 50, 74-5
diagnosis, 22, 46, 137-40, 151
Diagnostic and Statistical Manual (DSM), 137-40
Diagnostic Interview Schedule for Children (DISC), 38-9
Direct Observation Form (DOF), 118, 131-5
discriminant analysis, 55-8
drug therapy, 147

Edelbrock, C., 7, 12, 19, 24, 31, 38-40, 43, 46, 61, 70, 138, 144, 166-7
empirically-based assessment, 117-9, 137-40
epidemiological research, 144
etiological research, 145-7
Evans, W.R., 38, 167
externalizing, 31-5, 50, 52, 59, 110, 145, 161, 163

factor analysis & components analysis, 18, 31
factor loadings, 18-9, 21, 176-9
false negatives, 53, 55, 57
false positives, 53, 55, 57
family, 118, 121